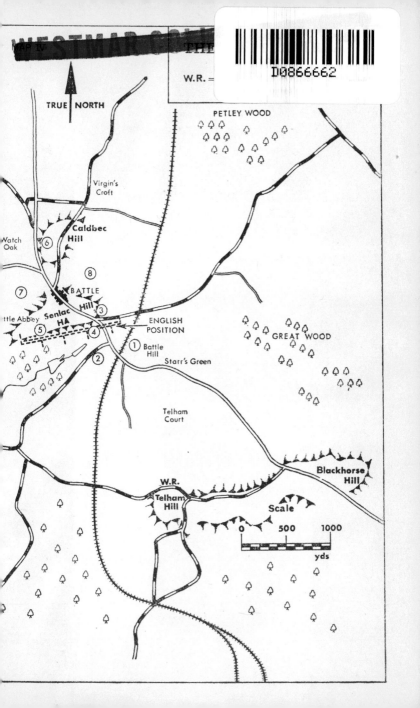

MAP IV WESTMAR THE

W.R. =

TRUE NORTH

PETLEY WOOD

Virgin's Croft

Watch Oak

Caldbec Hill
⑥

⑧

BATTLE Hill
⑦

Battle Abbey   Senlac HA   ③

⑤   ④   ENGLISH POSITION

① Battle Hill

②   Starr's Green

GREAT WOOD

Telham Court

W.R.
Telham Hill

Blackhorse Hill

Scale

0   500   1000

yds

The course of history might have been very different if Harold had been victorious instead of William at Hastings in 1066. Better or worse?—we don't know—but most certainly different. That is the measure of this battle's crucial importance. William's victory sharply changed the course of England's destiny, and in doing so no doubt shaped many basic developments all over the world in the centuries to come. In the ninth centenary year it is fitting that this full, informative and authoritative account should be made.

Brigadier Barclay begins with background information about pre-Conquest England, and shows how events during the twenty years preceding the final overthrow of the Saxon thanes brought about the Norman invasion and influenced the battle, and then gives fuller treatment than has been attempted before to the preparations on both sides in the few months prior to the conflict. The description of the battle itself is based on the known facts, supplemented by probabilities which have been worked out by the author from his own historical and military knowledge and from many visits to the battlefield itself.

The book ends with some speculations—which the author emphasises are no more than well considered surmises—on the probable effect of the Norman invasion.

The text is illustrated by a number of maps and plates, including an aerial photograph of the battlefield as it exists today. An appendix contains useful information for those who may wish to visit Hastings and the battle-field.

Brigadier C. N. Barclay

was commissioned in the Cameronians (Scottish Rifles) in 1915. He served in France and Mesopotamia during World War I and on the North-West Frontier of India in 1919. Service in China was followed by graduation at the Staff College, Camberley, in 1930 and further service in India.

During the second World War he was in command of an infantry bat-talion at Dunkirk, and a Brigade in North-West Europe in 1944-45. He also served on the Staff in South-East Asia. Since his retirement soon after the war he has devoted his time to military writing. He is editor of *The Army Quarterly and Defence Journal* and the author of many books and articles on regimental and military history.

This extensive military and literary experience, combined with his detailed study of the Hastings battlefield, pro-vide Brigadier Barclay with exceptional qualifications to write *Battle 1066*

BATTLE
1066

Brigadier C. N. Barclay,
C.B.E., D.S.O.

with 4 pages of plates and 4 maps

D. VAN NOSTRAND COMPANY, INC.
PRINCETON, NEW JERSEY

© Text, Brigadier C. N. Barclay, 1966
© Maps, J. M. Dent & Sons Ltd, 1966
All rights reserved
Printed in Great Britain
at the
Aldine Press · Letchworth · Herts

D. VAN NOSTRAND COMPANY, INC.
Princeton · New Jersey

First published 1966

ACKNOWLEDGMENTS

I owe all my basic knowledge to the old Chroniclers, and those who designed and made the Bayeux Tapestry, to whom I express my humble gratitude.

I also wish to make known my indebtedness to the more modern writers whose works are mentioned in Appendix B.

My thanks are due to Mr H. H. Lamb, of the Meteorological Office, Bracknell, Berkshire, for his advice on meteorological matters; and to the authorities of the National Portrait Gallery, London, who advised and helped me to obtain the only contemporarily produced likenesses of the three kings—Edward, Harold and William —in existence, and which are reproduced on Plate 1.

I must also acknowledge my indebtedness to Mr J. Manwaring Baines, the curator of the Public Museum and Art Gallery, Hastings, for his help and advice, and to Group Captain Ralph Ward, the Organizer of the Nine Hundredth Anniversary Celebrations, who briefed me on local matters on occasions when I visited Hastings and the battlefield area.

The photographs facing page 18 are reproduced by permission of the National Portrait Gallery, and that facing page 35 by permission of Aerofilms Ltd. Plate 3 is reproduced from *The Bayeux Tapestry*, edited by Sir Frank Stenton, published by Phaidon Press Ltd, London.

C. N. B.

January 1966.

CONTENTS

Author's Preface, ix

vii

MAPS

AUTHOR'S PREFACE

It is difficult to assess with accuracy the influence on history of any particular event, and not easy to say with certainty that any one episode outweighs all others in importance. But, looking back over the centuries in this nine hundredth anniversary year, we can state with confidence that the victory of William of Normandy over Saxon Harold at Hastings in 1066 was one of the very great landmarks.

Feudalism, of a kind, had existed in England before the Conquest, but that introduced by William was more centralized and much more efficient. Without this particular form of Norman feudalism, and the generally vigorous rule of the Norman and Plantagenet kings, progress and national development in England would have been much slower—how much slower we cannot say. It may be that the great overseas adventures which, much later, brought us our Empire would have been carried out by others. India might have fallen to France and North America become French, Spanish or Portuguese. Who knows who would have occupied Australia and New Zealand? Similarly the colonization of Africa would almost certainly have been very different. All this is surmise, but it is not far-fetched.

Although we cannot see the exact pattern of history as it might have been, it is tolerably certain that the world of the eighteenth and nineteenth centuries, and today, would have been very different if the Norman Conquest had not taken place. If we think along these lines we see what a momentous affair it was that took place in Sussex on 14th October, some nine hundred years ago.

The events described in this book occurred at a time when few people outside the priesthood could read or write, and what they wrote could only be reproduced on the smallest scale and very laboriously. It requires little imagination to appreciate the difficulties under which the old writers worked; how hard it was for them to acquire true and unbiased information and, having got it, how hard it was for them to present it in a manner which would be acceptable to the very limited number of people who would read it.

Most accounts of military operations were written after the event, many outside the lifetime of the participants. A number of factors contributed to make these accounts unreliable: the natural desire of the writers to produce a good story from scanty information led, one suspects, to much exaggeration and a lot of guessing. Stories of battles were invariably written by a partisan of one side or the other, and often by one with a personal attachment to a particular leader. In the atmosphere of the eleventh century we could hardly expect William of Poitiers, who was the Conqueror's chaplain and author of one of the best known accounts of Hastings, to write an entirely unbiased version. Hero-worship often led to gross bias and inaccuracies and, because of this, many authorities regard accounts written some years after the event as more reliable than contemporary records. There was also the common human tendency to exaggerate numbers, and it is a characteristic of many of the old chroniclers that their estimates of battle strengths and casualties were often fantastically high. Any numbers above a few hundred seem to have conveyed as little to medieval society as do the astronomical 'light years' of scientists to the average person today.

I do not accept an account merely because it is based on the stories of eye-witnesses, or even if the writer himself was an eye-witness. It was the fashion of the times to embellish the accounts of great events according to the writer's sympathies or self-interests. The military historians of recent events have access to carefully compiled and meticulously edited war diaries, written up from day to day. Private diaries and letters, reports by journalists and numerous other means add to the fund of information available in a society which is almost one hundred per cent literate. Having drafted his account the twentieth-century writer can send copies round to those best acquainted with the events, and in this way they can be checked and rechecked. In our free democracy a writer can, within reasonable limits, speak his mind without fear of unpleasant consequences.

Nevertheless, with all these advantages, inaccuracies still occur—sometimes very glaring ones—usually by mistake, occasionally by intent. Even the official historians with their unequalled sources of information, adequate staffs and leisurely methods are sometimes in error, although the British official histories are, as one would expect, of a very high order of accuracy.

If mistakes occur in accounts of recent happenings, how much more likely and excusable are they in those written long ago. In the eleventh century there were no war diaries and practically no personal documents. The historian had to get his information verbally, often through mere gossip. His writing could only be checked by others with difficulty —in an age when there were no printing-presses or type-writers and most people could not even sign their names.

For these reasons I accept with caution the details of events as recorded in early times. In the case of Hastings we know the basic facts—where the battle took place, who won and lost and the names of fatal casualties among the leaders. The rest is a matter of possibility, probability and reasonable surmise.

The Hastings battle—including the years before and after —is better documented than many historical events of similar antiquity. The *Anglo-Saxon Chronicle*—maintained from the ninth to the twelfth centuries—is a very complete background record, although not of much value for the actual battle. In some of the old battles not even the site is known with certainty; but that at Hastings is accurately marked by the ruins of William's abbey. Nevertheless, no writer could hope to complete a book of this sort based solely on established facts. If he tried he would not get much beyond a short magazine article and it would make very dull reading. Reasonable assumptions must be made and legend, if in the realm of probability, should not be despised.

In describing military operations I have based my conclusions on what, from my own military knowledge and experience, I regard as likely. A good example is Harold's dispositions at Hastings. We know the site of the battle and we have a good idea of the strength and composition of the English army; but we do not know with certainty the exact frontage and dispositions adopted. The various authorities differ very widely in their views and some are so tactically unsound as to give the impression that Harold was an incompetent amateur as a war leader. In fact we know that Harold was a very able and experienced commander. It therefore seems reasonable to assume that he made good use of the ground and disposed his force to the best advantage. From this we can hazard a good guess at the layout adopted, which is probably not far short of the truth. This is the way I have worked. Known facts are given as such; but, in the much more frequent cases where the course of events is doubtful, I have indicated that there *is* doubt and given what I believe to be a reasonable and likely story.

At first sight it appears logical to suppose that those who wrote nearer the event were more likely to be correct in their facts and assumptions than more recent historians. I do not think this is the case. The intelligent modern writer has so many advantages over the old chroniclers—access to all the literature available and an open mind which need not be swayed by sentiment or allegiance. Moreover, it is no longer the fashion to idealize: the modern biographer does more harm than good to his subject if he indulges in unwarranted hero-worship. The trend is to find the truth and state it impartially. In the case of the battle of Hastings the modern writer has the Bayeux Tapestry, which was not available to the majority of the old chroniclers. These advantages, combined with the application of a trained military mind, are, I suggest, a guarantee of reasonable accuracy—but not of infallibility.

Finally, I would emphasize that the book is primarily for the general reader, rather than for scholars of the period —although I would not wish to discourage the latter from reading it! I have not cluttered the pages with lengthy foot-notes or source references; nor have I used fifty words if I think fifteen will suffice. I have written for the average well-educated and inquisitive man or woman who takes an interest in our country's story.

C. N. BARCLAY.

London,
January 1966.

I

Britain and Normandy
before the Conquest

See Map1

BRITAIN

When the Romans withdrew from Britain at the beginning of the fifth century they left a situation not unlike that in a few ex-colonial territories today. For nearly four hundred years the country had been policed and protected by Roman legions, and administered by a Roman bureaucracy. Little attempt had been made to educate the native inhabitants or fit them to govern themselves. That the necessity for doing so would ever arise was not contemplated in the heyday of Rome. Those Britons who participated in the administration did so in subordinate positions and on a local basis. Outside the few large towns, and away from the main highways, the inhabitants remained little more than tribal savages.

With the departure of the Roman administration and the legions the country was not only thrown into confusion, but the way was opened for many warlike invaders from overseas who had long cast covetous eyes on this pleasant land. The sea, later to become our sure shield and protection, was the highway of those days—a much easier one than the roadless forests, swamps and mountains of most of continental Europe. Without a navy, unorganized and with a

population too small to guard her long coastline, the
Britons of the post-Roman era fell an easy prey to the
raiders, and later settlers, from Scandinavia. Moreover, the
fierce Britons whom Caesar had first encountered in 55–54
B.C. had probably become 'soft' under long Roman protection and were less capable of defending themselves than
their warlike ancestors, though the Arthurian legend
suggests that, when a good local leader did arise, resistance
could be prolonged and temporarily effective.

G. M. Trevelyan regards the settlement of the Nordic [1]
people as the primary event in British history. The story
begins during the last century of Roman occupation, when
Saxon raiders made frequent tip-and-run excursions to our
shores, and ended in the beginning of the eleventh century
some years before the Norman conquest. We have little
knowledge of these early invaders. Some were apparently
first invited by local British chieftains, to help the latter
fight the marauding Picts, subsequently turning against
their employers, and conquering the areas they had come
to help. Amongst the first were the Jutes, who began
settling in the south-east of the island about 449 under
Hengist and Horsa and within a few years had established
the kingdom of Kent under Hengist. Another Germanic
tribe was the Angles, who gave their name to the country—
England, the land of the Angles. The first Saxons to arrive
as settlers probably did so about 477, but a more serious
invasion under Cerdic apparently took place around 495.
In fact we know little about Hengist, Horsa and Cerdic.
They, and many other names of the period, are not

---

[1] Nordic. The word is used to cover all people of Scandinavian and
north German origin who came to settle in England—Angles, Saxons,
Jutes, Danes, etc.

legendary in that we know they existed and we know the general pattern of their exploits, but many of the details of their activities, as taught to Victorian schoolchildren, are fiction.

It must be emphasized that the fifth- and sixth-century Saxons who came to Britain were very different from the Nordic invaders of earlier times. They were mostly farmers, with some degree of agricultural skill, seeking a better land than their own, with a more temperate climate.

By the end of the sixth century the major part of Britain had been settled by Saxons. The Britons had been driven into the western part of the island in three groups—Strathclyde, embracing the west coastal regions of southern Scotland and northern England; the Welsh mountain region (roughly modern Wales) and west Wales (roughly modern Cornwall). But Saxon Britain was far from being homogeneous: it comprised seven separate kingdoms known as the Heptarchy—Wessex, Sussex, Kent, Essex, East Anglia, Mercia and Northumbria. These little kingdoms were often at war among themselves and with the Welsh.

By the end of the eighth century the Saxon settlers had lost most of their seafaring skill. They were farmers, settled in the hinterland of the country; not exactly tribal, but living in small communities. The Anglo-Saxons were the pioneers of village life and parish administration, as it still exists in some parts of the country. Apart from the fairly frequent wars between rival kingdoms, and on the Welsh borders, life was humdrum. The people had become hard-working men who preferred peace to war. In these conditions it was not surprising that others, living in bleak and less congenial lands, should hear of the delights of Britain and cast envious glances in her direction. These were the

Danes, who from very early times had raided Britain, and whose ferocity and ruthlessness had become legendary. By the end of the eighth century the Danes were to change from raiding to settlement and colonization, and in little more than two hundred years a Danish king was to rule all England.

Before telling the story of the Danes it will be as well to describe briefly the progress of Christianity in England, which had begun under the Romans, but with the coming of the pagan Saxons had for all practical purposes only survived in Wales and the extreme south-west. Later Christianity was adopted by the Anglo-Saxons. The first abbey in the country had been founded at Bangor in 560; in 565 Christianity was being preached among the Picts and in 602 and 604 respectively the Archbishopric of Canterbury and the See of London were founded, as a direct result of St Augustine's mission to Kent from Rome in 597. By the end of the eighth century the Christian religion was firmly established in nearly all Britain, but was to receive a setback with the arrival of the pagan Danes.

The Danish invasion, as distinct from raids and plundering expeditions, may be said to have started in the closing years of the eighth century, and by the time Alfred the Great became king in 871, the Danes had occupied the greater part of the country north of a line stretching from Chester to the mouth of the Thames, this area being known as the Danelaw. The Saxons, in their effort to restrain the Danes, resorted to measures which closely resemble what today we call 'appeasement'. They tried to buy off the Danes with cash, and in this way the word 'Danegeld' was introduced into our language—a word which is still used occasionally in connection with blackmailing activities.

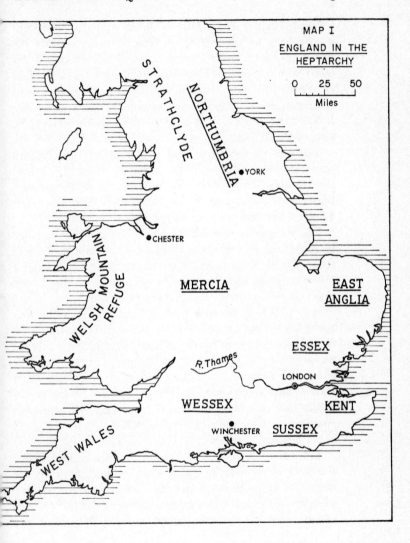

MAP I

ENGLAND IN THE HEPTARCHY

0   25   50
Miles

STRATHCLYDE

NORTHUMBRIA

● YORK

● CHESTER

WELSH MOUNTAIN REFUGE

MERCIA

EAST ANGLIA

ESSEX

R. Thames

LONDON

WESSEX

KENT

● WINCHESTER

SUSSEX

WEST WALES

In 825 Egbert had subdued Mercia and established the overlordship of Wessex. Egbert has often been styled the first king of all England, but in fact his influence outside his own realm was small. Following Alfred's defeat of the Danes at Ethandune his successors, Edward the Elder and Athelstan, consolidated the supremacy of Wessex, and when Edgar came to the throne in 959 he could justly claim to be king of all England.

The end of the tenth and beginning of the eleventh centuries were notable for the unhappy reign of Ethelred the Unready. New Danish raids along the south and east coasts took place, and the whole of south and south-east England became the scene of plunder and massacre.

The incapacity of Ethelred, and his deposition in 1013, increased the power of the Danish English and resulted in three Danish kings ruling the country—Canute, Harold I (Harefoot) and Hardicanute. In 1042, however, the Saxon line was restored with Edward the Confessor.

It is well to remember that in England monarchy had never been regarded as strictly hereditary. The main factor was acknowledgment by the Witan. Its members preferred an hereditary king, but they were prepared to pass him over if he was unsuitable, as they did when they appointed Canute and later Harold II. The part played by the Witan in this matter is important, as it crops up again when we come to consider the rival claims to the throne of Harold and William of Normandy.

This summary is intended to give, in the briefest terms, the story of the Nordic invasion of England, between the departure of the Romans and the unification of the country to form one state. We now come to the period of two decades —the reign of the Confessor—immediately before the battle of Hastings. The events of those years led up to, and may be said to have caused, the battle and they merit closer study.

The death of Hardicanute in 1042 gave the English the opportunity to shake off Danish rule by proclaiming as their king Edward (later called the Confessor), the son of Ethelred the Unready and Emma the daughter of Richard I, Duke of Normandy. The choice of Edward was strongly supported by Earl Godwin, at that time the most powerful magnate in the country, who no doubt saw him as a weak character who offered him an opportunity to enhance his own already powerful position.

Although the accession of Edward brought Danish supremacy to an end, in the long run it was to pave the way for a new conqueror—William of Normandy. The new king was Norman on his mother's side, had spent much of his early life in Normandy and spoke French as his first tongue. He was a devout Christian but a poor king. He showed little political sense and lacked any military skill or zeal—in an age when the chief duty of a king was military leadership.

Mainly because of the personality of its king, England in the twenty-four years before Hastings made little progress towards closer unification. The King's only positive act of policy during his reign was to introduce Normans into Church and State. He is remembered chiefly as the founder and builder of Westminster Abbey.

What of the country itself, its people and their way of life?

It is not easy to define the position of the Witan, or Council of Wise Men. It has sometimes been called the first English Parliament, but that is incorrect. It was not an elected, or even a representative, body, but a collection of nominated earls, leading churchmen and other notables. Its nearest equivalent in modern times is probably the Privy Council. It based its authority mostly on custom, and one of its main duties was to select or confirm a new monarch. This it seems to have done with considerable success, except perhaps in the case of the Confessor. Throughout his reign the great earls, and the Norman prelates and notables whom he introduced, largely usurped the functions of both monarch and Witan.

Towards the end of the period before Hastings London resumed its important role as the chief port for trade with the Continent, which had been dormant since Roman times. Other cities and towns such as Canterbury, Salisbury, Winchester, Norwich, York and Durham were increasing in importance and size, partly as ecclesiastical centres and partly as markets for the exchange of goods and for general commerce. But in the main the estimated population of $1\frac{1}{2}$ million were farmers, tilling the land to feed themselves and lumbering the forests for their own local purposes. As a generalization it can be said that the Danes tended to concentrate in the towns and along the east coast, and the Saxons in the inland country districts. Under the great earls were the overlords, usually a bishop or abbot: next came the king's thegns and under them the peasants. The thegn was roughly the equivalent of the Norman knight and spent his life in hunting, making or preparing for war, and administering justice. Although the peasant was no doubt dependent on his thegn to a very great extent he was, under this very mild form of Saxon feudalism, a comparatively free man. He was liable to be called out for military duty for forty days a year, but one suspects that he was a somewhat inefficient soldier who did very little training for war when not actually mobilized. Unlike the thegn his interest was in agriculture, not in soldiering.

One cannot over-emphasize the great part played by the Christian Church and the awe in which the great Church dignitaries were held. Men who would perpetrate the most shocking cruelties on prisoners of war and others within their power, nevertheless regarded an oath, given under the customary rites of the Church, as absolutely binding. Men of position and wealth would undergo most rigorous penances at the behest of a Church dignitary. Poor communities, only just able to scratch a living from the soil, nevertheless built magnificent abbeys and churches, which in beauty of design and quality of workmanship cannot be approached today. This among people who had in many cases been Christians for perhaps only a few generations. There are still in existence in England more than four hundred churches which can be identified as pre-Conquest Anglo-Saxon in origin. Such was the power of the Church of Christ nine hundred years ago.

We now come to one of the most important and interesting features of the Confessor's reign—the introduction of Norman influence into Britain. Due no doubt partly to his Norman upbringing, and because he was French speaking, the King imported leading Normans into the Church and Court, one of the first being Robert, Abbot of Jumièges, who became Bishop of London in 1044 and Archbishop of Canterbury in 1051. Another reason may have been Edward's desire to offset the influence of Godwin, who, having been mainly responsible for placing him on the throne, was inclined to demand an undue share in the affairs of state. Whatever the cause, the fact remains that by the end of the Confessor's reign Norman influence was very strong. This was particularly the case in south-east England, where William's army landed. Like others some nine centuries later, in other parts of the world, they had established, by a process of infiltration, a dangerous 'fifth column'. We do not know to what extent William of Normandy encouraged this; but it seems highly likely that, during the latter years of Edward's life, the Duke was not unmindful of the advantages of a strong Norman element in Britain if he had to fight for the crown which he believed to be his right. It would appear that although the Conqueror received only a limited amount of direct help from his countrymen domiciled in England, either before or at Hastings, it proved of great advantage during the process of consolidation after Harold's defeat. Without this help it is unlikely that he would have gained a kingdom as a result of a single battle.

Summarizing the twenty-four years of the Confessor's reign we can say that, by his indirect form of government and the Norman influence which he introduced, he created conditions which materially assisted the Conqueror in his conquest and consolidation of Britain. That he did this unwittingly, and not in any way in league with William, is shown by his nomination of Harold to be his successor. He seems to have been a man who could not read the writing on the wall.

NORMANDY

We can now turn to the consideration of the dukedom of Normandy, whose ruler was to bring about such a change in the story of England.

We first hear of the Normans, or Northmen, as pirates and raiders. In origin they were much the same as the Danes, and they came from the lands now known as Scandinavia. But the settlers from the north did not all go to England; some settled on the other side of the Channel where, in an amazingly short time, they developed characteristics of their own which were in many ways very different from those of their kinsmen settled in Britain.

The general trend of events, however, followed much the same pattern as it had done in England. By the first decade of the tenth century there were signs that the Northmen intended to substitute settlement for raiding. In 912 Rollo the Ganger and his followers seized an area of land around Rouen from Charles the King of the West Franks. By arrangement between the two, Rollo promised to become a Christian, do homage to Charles and carry out some other formalities which were honoured more in their breach than in their observance. Rollo, assisted by his son William Longsword, soon began adding to his territory as more immigrants continued to arrive. Very soon his domain embraced the towns of Avranches, Lisieux and Caen. In this manner was founded the dukedom of Normandy.

Again the general pattern of events was much the same as in England. The original settlers arrived as warriors, knowing no form of settled government. As with the Danes among the Saxons in England they began to adopt the customs of their new country, and quickly—more quickly than the Danes in England—they were assimilated by the French inhabitants around them. The process was indeed remarkably rapid. By the end of the reign of the third duke (Richard the Fearless, 943–96) the inhabitants of Normandy were all French speaking and had all embraced the

Christian faith. Their conversion to Christianity was of particular significance, because the process of Norman infiltration into England in the two decades before Hastings was largely the work of the Church.

The story of invasion is usually the story of the invader imposing his way of life and his skills on the subject race. In Normandy the reverse was the case, and the invaders proved very receptive. They learnt the art of continental warfare and soon developed, and improved upon, the techniques of the mounted armoured knight and the forti-fied castle. Moreover, they quickly acquired a veneer of French culture, especially in architecture—the construction of church buildings in particular. In less than one hundred years the Normans changed from a race of semi-savages into a cultivated, well organized people. They seem to have done this without losing their Viking enterprise and hardihood.

This was a much quicker pace of development and pro-gress than that of the Saxon-Danish population in England who, by the early years of the eleventh century, were still a primitive people devoted to agriculture, fishing and rural crafts, and versed only in the age-old methods of war. This, as we shall see, was to be an important factor in the events of 1066.

It was during the reign of Richard the Fearless that Hugh Capet founded the French monarchy, by a process of conquest in which he was assisted very considerably by Richard. This resulted in the Duke of Normandy becoming the vassal of the French king.

The reign of the fourth duke, Richard the Good, was notable for a number of events which later had considerable impact on the English scene. In 1002 the English king,

Ethelred the Unready, married Richard's sister, Emma. Their son was to become Edward the Confessor, and it was due to his Norman mother that Edward spent most of his early life in Normandy and spoke French as his mother tongue. This influence, as we have seen, was to result in the introduction of Normans to high office in England in the years before Hastings. The fourth duke's reign was also remarkable for the fact that the Normans began to establish an aristocracy and, for the first time, we begin to hear the names of those noble families who later played such a big part in English history.

On Richard's death in 1026 the dukedom was divided between the two rival brothers, Richard III and Robert, but upon the former's death in 1028, Robert became duke of all Normandy.

Robert died in 1035 on his return journey from a pilgrimage to the Holy Land, leaving as his heir the eight-year-old William—who was to play such a great role in our country's story. It is necessary to point out here that the law of heredity was much more strictly observed in France than in England. Nevertheless in those days the accession of a minor was not without danger and often the cause of strife. Moreover, William was illegitimate, his mother being Arletta, the daughter of a tanner in Falaise. This, although not considered a very serious matter in Court circles at that time, was hardly an advantage when contending for a throne. But Robert, before his departure on pilgrimage, took the precaution of getting the leading nobles to swear allegiance to his son. As a result William's accession was not disputed. His minority was not, however, without its perils and his life was continually threatened. By this time Normandy had become a powerful semi-independent state and the French king began to show animosity and the urge to take advantage of William's minority.

William, however, was no ordinary young man, and by the time he was twenty had begun to take an active part in the affairs of his realm. A rising in the western part of the country was quickly quelled, and very soon his Court began to rival that of any in Europe in splendour and talent. He showed himself quite able to administer and control the feudal system on which his state was organized. This system, although highly organized, was much less centralized than that established in England by William after Hastings. He surrounded himself with many able men, including Odo, Bishop of Bayeux, his half-brother through his mother's marriage with Baldwin of Conteville, and William Fitz-Osborne. The Church flourished and was well rewarded for its loyalty. He twice defeated the French king, Henry, when he invaded Normandy, and in 1063 conquered Maine.

By the 1060's Normandy had become a powerful realm, well organized in Church and State and with a ruler who had proved himself an able leader in war and peace.

CONCLUSION

The foregoing brief description shows how England, and much later Normandy, developed after the fall of Rome and the withdrawal of the legions and Roman administration. It will not, however, have escaped notice that, whereas progress in England was slow, that in Normandy was, by comparison, dynamic. There were a variety of reasons for this. In England the settlers were not homogeneous. The rivalry between Saxons and Danes and the division of the country into small kingdoms retarded progress. The Saxons were by nature somewhat lethargic but, in course of time, they assimilated the Danes. In contrast the men who settled in Normandy, although very similar to the Danes, not only retained their own virtues of hardihood and energy, but, in a very marked manner, absorbed the best qualities of the French inhabitants of Normandy and learnt the customs and skills of other parts of Europe. In their efforts to keep their independence, and survive the threats of the French kings, they became a united race.

The Normans quickly became Continentals; the English remained Nordic and retained many of the characteristics of their ancestors. The English fought at Hastings as their forefathers had fought their little wars long before. The Normans had learnt the technique of the mounted knight who, like the panzers nearly nine hundred years later, swept all before him.

To these basic differences must be added the Norman influence in Britain in the Confessor's reign, which was a substantial factor in William's favour.

It is wrong to think of the Norman invasion as the conquest of England by Frenchmen of alien race. It was in reality the fusion of two branches of the Nordic races, whose origins had been very similar.

II

Personalities and Military Forces

See Map II

PERSONALITIES

EDWARD THE CONFESSOR
HAROLD II
WILLIAM, DUKE OF NORMANDY
(*sometimes called William the Bastard and later the Conqueror*)

The personality of a leader was much more important nine hundred years ago than it is in these days of universal franchise, committees and automation.

Wars were mostly dynastic in origin—perhaps under the guise of religion or some other moral issue, but in reality for the aggrandizement of an individual. It was the main function of kings and princes to lead in battle, and the result usually depended on the leader's courage and skill. In more modern times if the general is killed, or dies suddenly, the immediate issue is not affected. His soldiers probably first hear of it on the radio. In the eleventh century it was very different. The story goes that at Hastings the Norman ranks began to waver when it was thought that William had been killed, but that the situation was quickly restored when the Duke uncovered and rode down the line to show that he was alive and active. Conversely the death of Harold was the climax of the battle: the already dispirited English army melted away.

To get a proper grasp of events in those days a knowledge of the leading figures is essential—in this case Edward the

16

Confessor, Harold and William. Our knowledge is meagre; it was before the days of the publisher and the Sunday press, eager for the personal accounts of the great. Only the priesthood could write with facility and the habit of keeping diaries was yet to come. Nevertheless we know enough of these three leading figures in our story to form a general impression of the kind of men they were, their probable reactions in given situations and their influence on events.

Edward the Confessor was born at Islip in Oxfordshire about 1004. He was the son of Ethelred the Unready and Emma, daughter of Richard I, Duke of Normandy. According to *modern* laws of heredity his claim was indisputable: there was no successor to the throne to follow Hardicanute in the Danish line. The only possible rival was Edward, the son of Edmund Ironside; but this was an illegitimate line, as Ironside was only a natural son of their common father Ethelred. Although illegitimacy was not a fatal bar to succession in those days it did have *some* bearing on the matter. Moreover the rival Edward was far away in Hungary; whereas the Confessor had been established in England for some little time, having been brought over from exile in Normandy by Hardicanute, who treated him with generosity and respect.

Rules of succession in those days were not, however, based solely on heredity, which was only one of the factors concerned. Saxon influence had been growing with the realization that Hardicanute had no heir, and Edward had the backing of the powerful Earl Godwin. When therefore the leading men of the realm assembled in London on Hardicanute's death to select a successor the choice of Edward appears to have been unanimous.

We do not, of course, know details of the proceedings, but it may well be that Godwin's influence was decisive. As it turned out, in the long run no choice could have been more fatal for the Saxon cause; for, more than anything else in the twenty-four years of his reign, the Confessor was to prepare the way, unwittingly no doubt, for the Norman conquest.

The new king had few of the attributes considered necessary for leadership in those days. He was not a man of war, but a deeply religious scholar and philosopher—more suited to be a monk than a king. Early in his reign he was largely under Godwin's influence, and it may have been partly to offset this that Edward later began to introduce Normans into Church and State. This is a more likely reason than his Norman upbringing. There is evidence of his dislike of Godwin, whom he strongly suspected of being involved in the murder of his brother Alfred Atheling in 1036.

It can be said of Edward that he took some measures to improve law and justice, but his most marked personal characteristic was a desire to be left alone to pursue his religious life without involvement in distractions. He seems however, to have had a harsh, and even cruel, streak in his character. This is borne out by his shabby treatment of his mother—who after Ethelred's death had married Canute. It is not part of this story to tell how this wish for a quiet life was disturbed by Godwin and his sons, following the earl's banishment and attempted return by force. He died in 1053, not long after his reconciliation with the king, and this enabled Edward to pass the last years of his life in comparative peace supervising the construction of his new abbey of Westminster.

Edward died on 5th January 1066, having on his deathbed,

EDWARD, 1042–1066
silver penny 1065

HAROLD, January to October 1066
silver penny 1066

WILLIAM, 1066–1087
silver pennies of *c.* 1068 and 1068–71, respectively

PLATE 1.   THE THREE KINGS

Photographic enlargements of silver coins; actual diameter ¾in.
For further particulars see Appendix B.

so it is said, requested the Witan to choose Harold, Godwin's son, as his successor. Harold was not, however, without a rival, and before discussing the personal qualities of the two major figures of the Hastings battle it will be as well to examine these rival claims to the throne.

If we overlook the illegitimate origin of his grandfather (Edmund Ironside) there can be no doubt that the best claimant on an hereditary basis was Edgar Atheling. That the illegitimacy of his line cannot be regarded, by the customs of those times, as a serious bar is shown by the fact that after Hastings the Witan actually chose him to succeed Harold. He was never crowned and, of course, very soon gave way to the Conqueror. That he was not chosen in preference to Harold was due to his being a minor at the time.

Harold's claim on purely hereditary grounds was a poor one, in fact non-existent. His father, Godwin, Earl of Wessex, is said to have been the son of a herdsman. He could claim a royal connection on his mother's side, she being Gytha, grand-niece of Sweyn who had been King of Norway; but this gave him no valid claim to the English throne.

William's claim on hereditary grounds was better than Harold's, but he was, of course, illegitimate. He, however, claimed to be the Confessor's next-of-kin through the latter's mother Emma, who was the daughter of Richard I, Duke of Normandy.

On hereditary grounds alone the order of precedence was without doubt Edgar—William—Harold: but, as already explained, the throne of England had never been purely hereditary. In the final count it was selection by the Witan that mattered and, although descent was one factor, much more important ones were the suitability of the claimant

C

GENEALOGICAL TABLES

of the Three Claimants to the English Throne on the
Death of Edward the Confessor on 5th January 1066

EDGAR ATHELING

ETHELRED II ≠ ELFLEDA
(The Unready) | (a daughter of Ealdoman Thored)
978–1013 (deposed) and 1014–16

EDMUND II = EALDGYTH
(Ironside) (illegitimate)
April–November 1016

EDWARD ATHELING = AGATHA
(related to Henry II, Emperor)

EDGAR ATHELING

A minor in 1066. Claim discarded by the Witan in favour of Harold; but chosen king by the Witan on the death of Harold in October 1066.

HAROLD

GODWIN = GYTHA
Earl of Wessex | (grandniece of Sweyn,
(son of a herdsman) | King of Norway)

HAROLD II

Chosen king by the Witan on the death of Edward the Confessor. Killed at Hastings 14th October 1066.

WILLIAM

ROBERT ≠ ARLETTA
Duke of Normandy | (daughter of a tanner)

WILLIAM I
Duke of Normandy
(The Conqueror) (illegitimate)
1066–1087

OTHER RELATIONSHIPS

(a) Harold was Edward the Confessor's brother-in-law, the latter having married Harold's sister Eadgyth (Edith). They had no children.

(b) William was the Confessor's maternal cousin, through the latter's mother Emma, who was the daughter of Richard I, Duke of Normandy.

and his acceptance by the majority of the leading men in Church and State. Edgar, as a boy, was clearly not a suitable candidate in such troubled times. William, however, had a better case. He was a man of exceptional ability and energy, and he made claims on the grounds that Edward had named him as his successor—presumably when William visited England as Edward's guest in 1051 (or 1052)—and that Harold had sworn on oath acknowledging him as the rightful heir. Even if true—and it is quite likely that they were—these were promises which neither Edward nor Harold had the right to make. None of these claims carried much weight in England, where Anglo-Saxons, already highly suspicious of the Confessor's Norman associates, dubbed William a foreigner. They were, however, taken much more seriously in France and were important factors in gaining him support when he decided on an invasion of England.

Harold's claim was based on solid worth. He had proved himself a fine soldier and a man of energy and determination. Moreover he was the son of the great Earl Godwin, his sister was Edward's wife and his own wife was the daughter of Alfgar, Earl of Mercia.

In spite of Norman influence in high places the Witan, on Edward's death, seem to have had little hesitation in accepting the late king's advice and choosing Harold. By English custom he became the rightful king; there is no truth in the accusation, made by some writers, that he usurped the throne.

That, very briefly, sets out the rival claims to the English throne in January 1066. We can now examine the two leading figures in the drama which followed nine months later, and see what sort of men they were.

Harold was born about 1022 and was thus about forty-four years old when he became king. He seems to have inherited his father's better qualities of energy and good judgment, and in other respects was a worthy and likeable character. He was pious, had a keen sense of justice and was a fine leader in battle. If he had a fault it was impetuosity. In the wars against the Welsh he had greatly distinguished himself, particularly in 1063 when he planned and carried out a 'combined operation' by sea and land against Griffith of Wales, who had raided and plundered the west of England.

One day about 1064—the exact date is not known—Harold landed on the coast of Normandy. The usually accepted version, which accords with the Bayeux Tapestry, is that he was sent by the Confessor on a diplomatic mission. Another story is that he was sailing in the Channel and was driven by a storm on to the Normandy coast. Whichever version is correct, he was detained by the local magnate, one Guy of Ponthieu, who handed him over to William. To the Norman duke it must have seemed a heaven-sent opportunity to consolidate his position as heir to the Confessor's throne. He treated Harold with hospitality and respect, and introduced him to the Norman methods of warfare by taking him on a campaign against Count Conan of Brittany. The story goes that, as a condition for allowing Harold to return to England, William made him take an oath acknowledging him as Edward's successor. The oath was said to have been made more binding by the surreptitious concealment of the bones of some dead saints under the table at which the oath was taken. Whatever the truth of this story, William made a great point of it later when claiming the English throne.

William was born in 1027 or 1028 and was therefore some five or six years younger than Harold. As we have seen, he was illegitimate, but his father assured his succession as a minor by extracting a promise to that effect from the leading men in Normandy before proceeding on his fatal journey to the Holy Land. William turned out to be worthy of this confidence and displayed all the qualities required of a leader. At a very early age he took over the reins of government, and soon showed his prowess in the military field. He defended his realm with success, even against his overlord the King of France, and in addition to his conquest of England added considerably to his continental realm.

The two contestants were well matched in character and military prowess; but to complete the picture we must see what sort of forces they disposed—their weapons and methods of fighting.

ENGLISH AND NORMAN MILITARY FORCES

It is unnecessary to discuss in great detail the military systems, clothing, accoutrements and weapons of the rival armies; but some knowledge of these matters is required for a proper understanding of the Hastings battle.

ENGLISH

Harold's army consisted of two distinct elements—the housecarls (or regular household troops) and the shire levies.

The housecarls were mounted, but they were mounted infantry, not cavalry. They used their horses for mobility, but they always fought on foot. Their chief weapon was the bill, which consisted of a heavy axe-type blade with a shaft or handle about three feet long. It was wielded with both hands like an axe, which it closely resembled. As a secondary weapon they seem to have been equipped with a lance or spear, which could be thrown or used for thrusting. The housecarls also carried large shields and these, when on the defensive, would be placed immediately in front of a line of men, or held by them, to form an obstacle behind which they fought. This was the famous 'shield wall', frequently mentioned in the sagas and accounts of Saxon battles. In practice the shields were probably often supplemented by stakes, rocks and other locally found obstacles to an advancing enemy. The housecarls were not heavily armoured, but had some protection for their heads and light chain-mail for the protection of parts of their bodies.

The shire levies, or *fyrd*, consisted of the able-bodied men of the country, who could be called out for forty days each year in defence of the realm. The sheriffs of counties were responsible for organizing the various contingents and getting them to the place of assembly. As their sole means of movement was on their feet they rarely fought very far from their own shire, although they occasionally had to do so. The levies who fought under Harold against the Welsh, those who helped him to defeat Harald of Norway in the north just before Hastings, and those who fought at Hastings, were mostly different bodies of men. The shire levies had no special uniform, and one suspects that they fought in their everyday working clothes. Their weapons, one imagines, were very varied. A good proportion probably had bills, a few may have had spears and shields, but it is likely that many were armed solely with farm implements.

There is no reliable evidence that Harold's army possessed any archers, although some authorities state that he had a few.

The English do not seem to have possessed any particular tactical skill although, as we shall see, at Hastings Harold selected a good defensive position and made good use of the ground. Generally speaking, however, an English army of those days relied on solid worth in hand-to-hand fighting. Before Hastings they had always fought against opponents similarly armed, and with similar methods, and their battles were mostly 'slogging matches' without any tactical subtleties.

NORMAN

William's and Harold's armies at Hastings were of very different patterns; and the former was not even typical of a feudal Norman army. Many of the knights, and a good proportion of the men-at-arms, were not Normans, but adventurers from other parts of France, or even farther afield, who had been attracted to William by the prospects of plunder and grants of land in England if the expedition was successful. The Normans had a very similar system for their men-at-arms, or levies, as the English; and forty days was the recognized limit for military service in any one year. Obviously the English adventure would last more than forty days, so it would seem that the infantry soldiers, as well as the knights, were mostly volunteers. This is, however, only surmise: it may be that the Norman feudal system—which was far more exacting than the English—could impress men for more than forty days.

The Norman system of fighting was very different from the English. Unlike the housecarls their knights fought mounted. Although both men and horses were only lightly armoured, compared with the very heavily encased mounted knights of a later period, it can be said that they were the forerunners of the light tank and their successors the forerunners of the heavy tank. They were lightly armoured mounted spearmen designed to charge and rout the opposing force. Often this had to be done frontally; but, as we shall see later, they were trained to take advantage of a situation which permitted a flank attack. No doubt their effect on morale was considerable (as it was with the tank eight and a half centuries later), and the mere presence of masses of these formidable horsemen would shake the nerves of the English shire levies.

It is clear that the Norman foot-soldiers were better found than their English counterparts. The Bayeux Tapestry shows a group of them carrying large pear-shaped shields and each armed with a spear some five feet long. The mounted men also seem to have been equipped with a sword and a battle-axe, the latter a weapon similar to the English bill but with a much shorter shaft. I can find no evidence that these latter weapons were extensively used by the infantry.

The Normans also had a body of archers; how many we do not know, but one thousand seems a reasonable surmise. They were not armed with the long-bow (a weapon originated by the Welsh), but with a much smaller kind with considerably less range—probably 150 yards or less. These were intended to have a 'softening-up' effect on the defenders before the infantry attacked or the mounted knights charged. An arrow is said to have been responsible for wounding Harold, although he was actually killed with a sword or by spear thrusts from mounted knights.

COMPARATIVE STRENGTHS

There can be no absolute certainty about the strengths of the opposing forces; but we can discount the inflated figures which appear in some history books. Some of the most careful historians have estimated the Norman strength on the fact that there is good (although by no means conclusive) evidence that William had 696 ships available to transport his force—men, horses, equipment and supplies. One estimate, based on this, gives a strength of 3,600 cavalry and 7,400 infantry. Taking into account that garrisons were left at Pevensey and Hastings, and that there had been some wastage through sickness, this would give a figure of about 9,000 Normans engaged in the actual battle. This estimate was given by General James, who went into the matter very carefully, and was later accepted as being a very likely figure by Lieutenant-Colonel A. H. Burne, who did much research into the battle of Hastings. There is no evidence that William received any reinforcements from Normandy between the original landing and the battle.

The strength of the English force is much more difficult to estimate. The Norman chroniclers stress the vastly superior numbers of Harold's army, but it is the way of historians to emphasize the superior strength of the other side. My estimate of the frontage held by the English is about 1,100 yards, and it appears likely that in order to provide the traditional 'shield wall' that front line was occupied mostly by housecarls which, giving one man per yard, and say two hundred men as escort to the king and for other extraneous duties, would make about 1,300 or 1,400 housecarls in all. This seems a reasonable figure.

There is no possible means of judging with any degree of

accuracy the strength of the English shire levies. My own view, which is little more than a 'hunch', is that early on 14th October when the battle began there were probably no more than three or four thousand; but that as the day advanced, and men kept coming in, it may have risen to ten thousand. The mounted housecarls probably arrived on the battlefield on the afternoon before, but I cannot see how any but a small proportion of the shire levies could have covered the fifty-eight miles from London before the very late evening before, or the morning of, the battle. As we shall see later, it is unlikely that any left London before the 11th and it may well be that some did not do so until the 12th.

It is interesting to speculate on the respective quality of the two armies. In numbers they were probably about equal at the height of the battle. Except that the Normans possessed archers there was nothing much to choose between their actual weapons which, in many ways, were similar. The one great advantage possessed by William was that he had a large body of knights who fought mounted. These, in combination with the archers, could provide a system of fire and movement unknown to the English.

Whilst it is true that Harold and his men fought on their home ground, it is probable that this was more than offset by the greater time William's army had to settle down. Held up, supposedly by contrary winds, they spent several weeks on the Normandy coast waiting for favourable weather. They were to spend another fortnight in the Hastings area before joining battle. It would be surprising if William had not taken advantage of these two periods to train his troops, formulate a tactical doctrine and generally discuss coming events.

Harold had no such period of preparation. As related in the next chapter, no sooner had he finished his successful campaign against Harald of Norway than he had to hurry south to meet the new foe. The Norman duke fought with a fresh army which had been together for some two months. The English king fought with an army which had been marching long distances for several days and which, except for the housecarls, was mostly new to him.

III

Prelude to Hastings

See Map II

No study of the battle of Hastings can be complete without an account of the many crucial events which preceded the battle. This is not just interesting background information : it is essential for a proper understanding of the great event itself.

The story begins with an episode which took place soon after Harold returned from Normandy in 1064 (or 1065). His brother Tostig, who ruled Northumbria, had governed so harshly that the people had rebelled, and unceremoniously, and with some bloodshed, caused his flight from York, where he had resided. They then replaced him with Morcar, a son of Earl Algar, for long an enemy of Harold and the rest of the Godwin family. Harold was no sooner back from Normandy than Edward sent him north at the head of a considerable force to put down the rising and teach the Northumbrians a sharp lesson. Before joining battle with Morcar and the Northumbrians it seems that Harold suggested a conference. After some lengthy deliberations Harold was so impressed by the Northumbrian's story, and convinced of the disgraceful behaviour of his brother Tostig, that he eventually persuaded the King to confirm

Morcar as Earl of Northumbria. The story has an interesting side-issue in showing the extent to which popular opinion often prevailed in Saxon England. It also confirms the view that Harold was a man with a keen sense of justice.

Meanwhile the enraged Tostig had gone to Bruges to his father-in-law, Baldwin, Count of Flanders. There he collected shipping and sufficient forces to raid the south coast of England; but Harold, who had by then become king, drove him off. Tostig then raided the east coast near the Humber, but was again beaten off, this time by earls Edwin and Morcar.

It appears that, on hearing of Harold's succession to the English throne, the Duke of Normandy at once decided to fit out a military expedition to invade England and seize the crown. Apart, however, from the time required to collect shipping and troops and plan the expedition, a number of other measures were necessary, partly to ensure the success of the expedition, but also to safeguard his continental possessions while he was away on a venture which, under the most favourable circumstances, could hardly last less than several months.

In 1052 William, disregarding a papal inhibition, had taken as his wife Matilda, the daughter of Count Baldwin of Flanders. Fortunately for him this papal ban was lifted in 1060 and, mainly through the influence of the famous Hildebrand (later Pope Gregory VII), he was able to obtain the approval of Pope Alexander II for his English expedition. Alexander sent him a special banner which he had blessed and a ring said to contain some of St Peter's hair. Throughout continental Christendom the chance of bringing the notoriously independent English Church closer to Rome was welcome, and gave William's cause the appearance of a holy war. The French king was apparently not prepared to help directly, but very probably gave some form of undertaking not to molest William's territory while he was away. Baldwin promised all the help he could give. With marked diplomatic skill and energy the Duke laid his plans for safeguarding his realm and preparing the expedition.

By about the end of July or early August William had collected or constructed at various Norman ports some 696 ships suitable for a cross-Channel move in convoy. We do not know the exact size or design of these ships, but there are reasons for believing that they were similar to those of a later period of which we have more knowledge. It has been estimated that a fleet of this size could carry a force of about 11,000 men and 3,600 horses, together with a reasonable amount of equipment and sufficient supplies to tide over the period before local produce from the English countryside could be gathered in. William is also said to have taken with him two 'forts'—in sections, ready to put together on arrival. No details of these are available and it is very doubtful if they ever existed. It is much more likely that they were not sections of forts, but 'barricades' of a kind, perhaps used for the same purpose as the familiar 'knife-rests' of World Wars I and II. Nevertheless we should not altogether discount the story of a prefabricated 'strong-point'.

While these activities were going on along the Normandy coast, Harold, who had been given early warning of William's intentions, organized a look-out system along the south coast and collected forces with the intention of giving the Duke a hot reception. Little is known of these preparations, but obviously the bulk of his force must have consisted of shire levies from the southern part of the country, with housecarls near the most likely landing-places. On the other side of the Channel William—to his intense irritation we are told—was held up for several weeks by contrary winds. This, according to some chroniclers, caused considerable discontent among his followers, some of whom returned to their homes. To Harold this delay was to be even more disastrous. It was the time of haymaking and approaching harvest in southern England, the season in which the Saxon farmers gathered in their produce to keep man and beast alive during the winter. It does not require much imagination to picture the 'grousing' which went on among the men of this militia force who, like some of the air-raid wardens, fire-watchers and anti-aircraft gunners of our own generation, watched night after night and day after day for an enemy who never came. What we today call 'desertion' must have been rampant and no doubt as time went on Harold found his force dwindling. Some time about the first week in September the King was obliged to disband most of his force, leaving the south coast almost bare to the invaders. It was also unfortunate that at about the same time the English fleet—which in June, July and August had been patrolling off the south coast—ran out of supplies. As a result Harold was forced to send it round to London to revictual and refit.

This might not have been such a serious matter had Harold, and the housecarls, been able to remain in the south ready to call out the levies again, and deal with the situation, if William of Normandy landed. There was, however, another contestant in the field for the English throne and, although he failed dismally, and fatally for himself, it is probable that his action to implement his bid was the cause of Harold's defeat at Hastings.

The new enemy was Harald Hardrada, King of Norway.

He had no valid claim to the throne, except the potential
one of conquest—acceptable with better grace then than it
is today. He was, however, a formidable opponent: one of
the great warriors of the time.

To tell the story of the new threat to the English king we
must return to Tostig, Harold's brother, who had been so
ignominiously removed from Northumbria. Following his
abortive raids on the south and east coasts of England,
described earlier, he travelled round Europe seeking
support for further enterprises against England. During his
travels he went to Rouen, where he undoubtedly saw
William of Normandy. There is no definite evidence that
the Norwegian king's activities were in any way co-
ordinated with William's. Clearly the Norman duke would
be only too pleased to see Harold of England embarrassed;
but he would hardly have connived to put Hardrada on a
throne which he claimed as his own and which he was
preparing to seize.

The final act of Tostig's comings and goings and in-
trigues was that he put his proposals to strike at England to
Hardrada. If successful the Norwegian was to become King
of England, and presumably Tostig was to receive some very
special preferment. The latter doubtless made light of his
banishment from Northumbria and gave the impression
that many Englishmen would join the invaders.

The forces of Hardrada and Tostig joined up at the mouth
of the Tyne. Then in mid September they landed on the
Yorkshire coast and moved on York. From York earls
Edwin and Morcar advanced to meet them; but were
heavily defeated at Fulford on 20th September. Hardrada
and Tostig and their troops then entered York; but later
withdrew to Stamford Bridge, about seven miles from York.

PLATE 2.   THE BATTLEFIELD FROM THE AIR
Taken from the west. The thick white line shows approximately the English position; the arrows show the ground over which the Normans attacked.   HA = High Altar marking the spot where Harold died.

Harold on hearing of Hardrada and Tostig's invasion hurried north. The chroniclers have not been very explicit about the battle of Stamford Bridge, which was somewhat overshadowed by Hastings. Harold is believed to have arrived in York on 25th September, having with him some housecarls and levies from the northern shires which he had collected *en route*. He would also be joined by the survivors of the forces of the defeated earls Edwin and Morcar. The invaders appear to have been taken completely by surprise, and one account has it that those on the near bank of the River Derwent were decimated before they were able to assume battle formation. Those on the far bank were, however, able to put up some show of resistance before Harold's men could cross the river, and a bloody fight took place.

Henry of Huntingdon gives a picturesque story of a parley said to have taken place before the battle, in which Harold offered Tostig Northumbria, and when asked to state Hardrada's share replied: 'Six feet of the ground of England, or perchance more seeing that he is taller than other men.' This parley before battle is hardly consistent with the tactical surprise which Harold seems to have achieved and it is probably 'chronicler's licence' rather than fact.

The truth is that we know little of these events, except the fact that Harold of England won a signal victory. The King of Norway and Tostig were both killed and their forces destroyed. Most of their shipping was captured, and with it the Norwegian king's boy son Olaf. Contrary to the customs of the time Harold not only spared his life, but provided shipping to take him back to Norway. Olaf is said to have given an oath to remain on friendly terms with England for the rest of his life.

D

The influence of the battle of Stamford Bridge on that at Hastings, less than three weeks later, will be apparent. By a freak of fortune the weeks of contrary winds, which we are told infuriated William and delayed his expedition, acted to his advantage in a manner which he could hardly have foreseen. It drew off Harold and his housecarls to the north, and by Hardrada's death one of William's rivals for the throne was eliminated. The only result more advantageous for William would have been the death of both Harold and Hardrada at Stamford Bridge.

For Harold of England the result of the actual battle was of course very satisfactory. Once again he had shown himself a leader of exceptional ability. There is, however, another side to the matter. It is possible that his decisive victory in the north gave him an over-confidence which was not justified when faced shortly after by the Norman duke and his formidable mounted knights. This aspect will be discussed more fully later, but there is justification for the view that Harold was over-hasty in joining battle at Hastings before his army had gathered in full strength.

On 28th September 1066—three days after the battle of Stamford Bridge—William of Normandy sailed from St Valery with an army some ten thousand or more strong. He was fortunate in being able to land near Pevensey unopposed. His fleet of transports must have been very vulnerable; had he been opposed, the whole enterprise might have failed at the outset and posterity would never have heard of the Norman Conquest. Those who have experienced landings on 'open beaches' under modern conditions will realize the formidable task of landing some thousands of horses from ships not specially constructed as 'landing-craft', and without any of the modern equipment

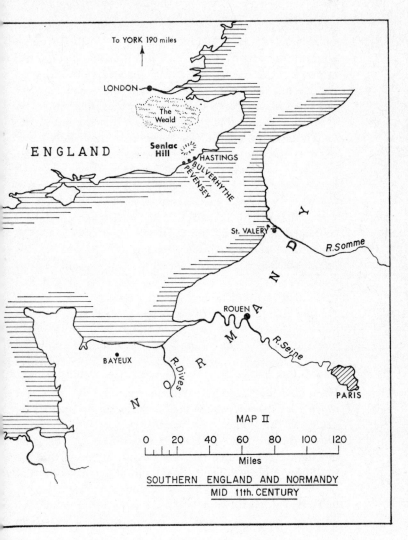

To YORK 190 miles

LONDON

The Weald

ENGLAND

Senlac Hill

HASTINGS

BULVERHYTHE

PEVENSEY

St. VALERY

R.Somme

NORMANDY

ROUEN

R.Seine

BAYEUX

R.Dives

PARIS

MAP II

0   20   40   60   80   100   120
Miles

SOUTHERN ENGLAND AND NORMANDY
MID 11th. CENTURY

which others—who invaded in the reverse direction 878 years later—enjoyed. We do not know how this and other administrative matters were handled. Probably a good deal of practice was carried out during the weeks of waiting on the Normandy coast; nevertheless it must have been a relief to William not to find an enemy awaiting him.

We can assume that the efficient Duke's first act was to send some of his foot-soldiers ashore to form a 'beach-head' to cover the disembarkation of the remainder of his men, the horses, equipment and supplies. This process may well have taken two or three days, and it is a reasonable assumption that very little local labour, voluntary or impressed, was available. Nor is it likely that the Norman contingent contained a large labour force for these purposes. The strength of the expedition was largely dictated by the amount of shipping available, and the Duke would want as many men as possible to be fighting men. The soldiers had to do their own unloading and other chores.

From the place of disembarkation the army moved almost at once to the vicinity of Hastings, where William made an entrenched camp. This was almost certainly on Castle Hill, probably near the site of the still existing ruins of Hastings Castle, built immediately after the invasion, Historians differ as to how William moved his men. A direct move from Pevensey along the coast was hardly practicable owing to the broken and marshy nature of the ground around Pevensey at that time. It might have been done by moving a considerable distance inland, although this too would have been difficult. Some authorities consider that the Duke re-embarked his force, but that seems highly unlikely. I think the most probable explanation is that the force did not land exactly at Pevensey, but a few miles nearer Hastings, at Bulverhythe. There the terrain was less difficult and it is believed that a move by land to Hastings would have been feasible.

The Norman horsemen rode far and wide from their coastal base, mainly one supposes in quest of supplies for men and animals, and as a protective measure to make certain that there was no large English force in the vicinity. In doing this they seem to have behaved with the customary barbarity of the times—killing the inhabitants and burning their farms and cottages.

It is a matter of speculation as to how much William was assisted by the Norman element in England for, although Normans had been excluded from the Court on the Confessor's death, many still remained in the country. One living near Hastings, named Robert Fitz-Wymara, is believed to have given him much information and advice, and it also seems certain that very soon after his arrival the Duke was well provided with information about Harold's movements and, in particular, the progress he was making to assemble an army in London.

We can now leave the Duke of Normandy and follow Harold's course of action.

The King is said to have received the news of William's landing while he was at York, celebrating his victory at Stamford Bridge. It is picturesque to imagine an excited horseman arriving while Harold and his close associates were feasting in some hall or public building. That may have been so, but we cannot be sure. Immediately his mind was made up: he would move at once to London to assemble and organize a force to meet the new invader.

We now come to some very interesting problems of time and space, and speculation on the nature of the army which assembled in the capital. The distance from York to London is about 190 miles and it is generally accepted that Harold left on 1st October and arrived in London six days later—that is on the 6th, or possibly the 7th if they started late on the 1st. That gives an average day's march of over thirty miles, for a mostly infantry army marching on its feet. I cannot credit that: my own picture is very different—based not on known facts but on what I believe a good and reasonable commander would do. It is something like this.

On hearing the news of the Norman landing—probably on the evening of 30th September—the King gave orders for the housecarls, the bulk of the thegns and other mounted men to be ready by dawn on the following day, 1st October. The marching personnel were to start about the same time, but would, of course, take longer to reach London than the King's mounted column. I believe the infantry column to have been very small. We do not know the exact composition of the shire levy element which fought at Stamford Bridge, or its strength, but it was mostly recruited from the northern and midland shires. Some of its members had been killed or wounded at Stamford Bridge, others may have already dispersed. I feel that only a very few—possibly only a few hundred—of the shire levies who took part in the northern victory fought also at Hastings.

The mounted column could, of course, have covered the distance in less than six days, but men and horses would be exhausted by their previous exertions and Harold let them take their time. In any case an average of about thirty-two miles per day for six days running, over indifferently kept roads and tracks, is not bad going for a considerable body of heavily laden horsemen. Moreover patrols and parties were probably used on the way down to gather in the shire levies of the south midlands and urge waverers to make haste. In other words, this was a form of 'recruiting march'. It also seems to me highly probable that the King and a small party rode on ahead of the main mounted column and reached London one or two days earlier, in order to get the latest information about William and arrange for the assembly of the levies as they came in. The infantry from York—very few in my opinion and probably moving in small parties—could hardly be expected in London before 8th or 9th October.

On about 10th October the situation was probably like this:

Normans. Still in their entrenched camp near Hastings and showing no signs of movement. Whether this was due to operational reasons, logistics or hesitancy on William's part will be discussed in the next chapter.

English. Harold and his crack troops—the housecarls— in London. The shire levies of East Anglia, the south midlands and southern England arriving in London in batches. Probably a few thousand had already reported. It is also recorded that the King ordered the fleet, which was refitting in the Thames, back to the south coast—presumably to cut off William's retreat and prevent the landing of reinforcements from Normandy.

Both Harold and William seem to have been very well informed about each other's movements. Some chroniclers state that during this period the two leaders discussed terms through their respective representatives. This would be in accordance with the custom of the times, but there are no reliable records of the nature of any parley which may have taken place.

These are the facts as far as they are known, supplemented by reasonable surmise. Subsequent moves of the two armies belong to the battle itself and are described in the next chapter. Before proceeding further there are, however, one or two points connected with what has already been written which merit comment.

WILLIAM'S DELAY OWING TO CONTRARY WINDS

Up to now historians have been almost unanimous in attributing William's long sojourn on the Normandy coast to contrary winds, and there is much evidence that it was so. He and his army are said to have become impatient, some of his original supporters so much so that they returned to their homes in disgust. Bad weather might set in and make the cross-Channel expedition too hazardous for the small craft of the day. In addition the arrival of severe weather in England might make serious campaigning impracticable and leave William and his army stranded in a hostile country for several months without the issue being decided. All this is true, but on the other hand the delay of some six weeks gave the Duke an opportunity to collect, or complete the construction of, more shipping and generally lay his plans more thoroughly than would have been possible had he set out in mid August when he is said to have been ready.

There is, however, another side of the matter which I do not think has been considered sufficiently. It has always been assumed that there was no collusion or co-operation between the Duke on the one hand and Harald of Norway and Tostig on the other. I believe that to be the case, as William would hardly have co-operated with a man who was a rival to the throne which he coveted. When, in addition, we consider the difficulties of communication, and the fact that military operations at that time were not conducted in accordance with precise schedules, I think we can definitely rule out any deep-laid plot between the two.

On the other hand I am not prepared to disregard the possibility that William knew about Hardrada's proposed plans and took advantage of them. It may not have been a complete fluke that the Normans landed only three days after the battle of Stamford Bridge. I think there is a good analogy in modern times. In the Suez affair in 1956 Britain and France did not actively co-operate with Israel; but they almost certainly knew of the proposed Israeli attack on Egypt and they made their own plans to dovetail in with those of Israel. I think it is possible—perhaps even likely— that William of Normandy acted similarly and that it was not entirely due to contrary winds that the invasion was delayed until the end of September. Whoever won the battle in the north, no harm—and probably much good— would come to the Norman duke if it synchronized with his own landing.

This view is to some extent reinforced by weather statistics concerning the customary conditions in the Channel at that time of year. The matter is considered in greater detail in Chapter V.

INTELLIGENCE AND COMMUNICATIONS

One must remember that in 1066 the fastest speed was that of a horse and, although very hardy, the horses of those days were not built for speed: it was before the days of flat racing and the English thoroughbred. I would put the average speed of relays of horsemen, changed perhaps every twenty-five miles, at not more than eight or nine miles per hour. From Pevensey to York is about 255 miles, which means that, barring accidents, and given an efficient organization, a message could have reached Harold in about thirty hours. But that would mean perfection and makes no allowance for drafting the message, mishaps on the way and finding Harold on arrival. In practice it would be good going if a message arrived in York within thirty-six hours and not surprising if it had taken forty-eight hours. The King received the message in time to leave York for London on 1st October, and as William did not land in England until probably the afternoon of the 28th it seems that Harold was well served by his 'Signals'. One can imagine that he made very special arrangements to ensure that he received tidings as quickly as possible of any untoward happenings along the south coast.

THE RIVAL PLANS

In the days when armies were mostly small the duration of a battle was rarely more than the hours of one daylight and the battlefield little bigger than a polo ground—at the most a golf course. Carefully worked out plans were unusual. There was no process of 'softening up' by cannon fire and air bombardment, no detailed reconnaissance, no air photographs or long briefings and orders at the various levels of command. Battles were *ad hoc* affairs, in which a plan was made up in a matter of minutes, implemented almost at once, and the result might well hang on some split-second decision by a quick-witted commander.

Nevertheless I feel that by about 9th October Harold and William must have formulated some ideas on how, when and where they intended to fight—what today we would call the 'strategic plan' or 'grand tactics'.

It has always been assumed that because Harold's army

consisted entirely of men who fought on their feet he had decided from the outset to fight the kind of defensive battle which he in fact fought. Similarly it is supposed by most historians that in view of William's large force of mounted knights—whose role was to attack—he intended taking the offensive.

I am not convinced that either of these assumptions is correct. It would be contrary to the character of the impetuous Harold to fight a defensive battle, and he had just won a great victory at Stamford Bridge by bold offensive methods. I think it much more likely that in a similar manner he intended trying to surprise William, who, he had heard, was entrenching himself at Hastings.

William's ideas are more difficult to fathom. I think it is quite possible that he had heard, in a general way, of what happened at Stamford Bridge, and that he thought that if he remained on the defensive Harold would repeat these tactics. Once Harold had battered his forces against the Norman defences, William would unleash his mounted men from some concealed position and give the *coup de grâce*. There is also some evidence that William, although a bold leader in battle, was strategically somewhat cautious; in which case he might have thought it good policy to fight near his shipping and after his opponents had just completed an exhausting march.

That, as I see it, is how the two leaders may have viewed the situation about 9th October—when Harold had been in London for some days and William was still at Hastings. As we shall see in the next chapter, circumstances arose which made necessary a drastic revision of both plans.

IV

The Battle

See Maps III and IV

PLANS AND PRELIMINARY MOVES

We have seen how on or about 9th October Harold was in London collecting his forces and William was at Hastings in a defensive camp. If the appreciation which I have already given is correct the King had every intention of advancing to Hastings and repeating the surprise attack which had proved so successful at Stamford Bridge a fortnight before. The Duke of Normandy had shown no signs of moving inland, and it is a fair assumption that he intended initially to stand on the defensive, using his powerful mounted force for a decisive counter-attack.

Now something occurred within the next few days which was to change what I believe were the original plans of the two leaders. It was Harold who was to stand on the defensive and William who did the attacking: it is interesting to examine how this came about.

As I have explained earlier, both sides seem to have been very well informed about each others' movements. Before going north, Harold had certainly made elaborate plans for keeping himself informed about the expected Norman invasion and the Duke's subsequent movements if he landed. William got local information from his mounted patrols, and doubtless his Norman friends resident in the country—his 'fifth column'—informed him of Harold's activities in London. Men's minds worked differently in 1066 to now; religion and superstition played a more prominent part; war was more a purely military matter, and less subject to political considerations; armies were less disciplined and the subordinate leaders and soldiers more likely to become disgruntled at inaction or, in the case of the Normans, if the spoils of war did not seem likely to come up to their expectations. Those with experience of modern war know how even the best disciplined troops, with all the amenities provided for a well-found force, can deteriorate through inaction. It is not difficult to imagine that William's knights—many of whom were not true Normans, but mercenaries from elsewhere—became impatient at what they regarded as the duke's hesitant policy.

In contrast Harold's natural impetuosity was probably accentuated by his recent victory. He would have received reports of the destruction by William's men of farms and villages in southern England. Although reason suggested delay to build up his forces, his whole inclination was to press on at once and deal with William of Normandy as he had with Harald of Norway.

That seems to me the likely states of mind in the two camps and, on this basis, I find it possible to give what I believe may be the true picture of how and why the two leaders came to reverse their original strategic plans.

About 9th or 10th October William probably received word from his spies in London that Harold was massing a huge force which, if allowed to collect unmolested, and given time to organize and settle down, would confront the Normans with overwhelming numbers. This news would

lend force to the arguments of the impatient knights who
had been pressing for early action. It would also be the
argument of Odo, Bishop of Bayeux, William's half-brother,
a reputed 'fire-eater'. As a result of these arguments the
Duke may well have decided to march north within the next
few days. The force would be alerted and all preparations
for an advance put under way.

At the same time some hard thinking and argument was
going on in London. Some counselled caution and advised
the assembly of an overwhelming force before offering
battle. Bolder spirits would point to the importance of
advancing on Hastings at once, before the Normans had
properly settled down in the country, completed their
defences and received reinforcements from the Continent.
The last of these points is one which must have weighed
heavily with Harold, although it has not been given
prominence by historians. But the King, if I judge him
correctly, was not the kind of man to be easily persuaded.
He liked to make up his own mind and he preferred a bold
course to inactivity. Harold therefore decided to move on
Hastings as quickly as possible with the forces he had got
and not to wait for all the shire levies to come in.

Although the decisions of the two leaders were very likely
made about the same time I think that Harold was quicker
off the mark and, if this is accepted, it explains a great deal.
Before continuing it is necessary to draw attention to the
fact that the country between the southern outskirts of
London to just north of the Senlac Hill and Stream (where
the battle took place), known as the Andredsweald (or
Weald), was then dense forest. It was traversed by a single
main road from north to south and no doubt many minor
tracks branching out from the main highway. Just north of

Senlac Hill the thick forest ended and open downs began, but not entirely devoid of trees and an occasional small wood or copse.[1] I think it was Harold's intention to push his army through the Weald as quickly as possible and occupy a position on Senlac Hill—not with the intention of fighting the battle there, but as a covering position behind which he could concentrate the main body of his force and give them a little rest preparatory to moving against William in his entrenched camp near Hastings. That seems to me a plan in keeping with the King's character.

The distance from London to Senlac Hill is about fifty-eight miles, and it is claimed by some historians that the English army did not leave London until 12th October to start the battle early on the 14th. I find this very hard to believe, and if it was so it goes a long way towards explaining Harold's defeat. Some years ago I discussed this with the late Lieutenant-Colonel A. H. Burne, who I mentioned earlier as a keen and thoughtful student of this battle. He was of the opinion that the King and his army left London on the 11th.

My own view is slightly different. I believe that Harold and the mounted portion of the army—the housecarls and various thegns and other leaders—went on ahead, probably leaving London on the 11th or 12th, overtaking and passing any parties of marching men who had already started, and arriving at Senlac Hill on the 13th, probably in the morning. This is some hours earlier than is given in most accounts. It explains how William received news of the English arrival and dispositions in sufficient time to advance and

[1] The line of demarcation between forest and down now hardly exists. It is not indicated on any modern maps, but is faintly discernible on air photographs.

deploy his force in an orderly manner by the early morning of the 14th. He was to achieve the dream of every general, before and since, of catching his opponent before he had time to deploy for battle, and defeating him in detail.

By the evening of the 13th the first of Harold's marching shire levies would begin to arrive, and they continued to arrive in batches throughout the night. Meanwhile William had heard what was going on and resolved to attack as early as possible on the 14th. All would be bustle and excitement in the Norman camp: the great moment, for which they had all been waiting, was at hand. Some time during the night, possibly about midnight, Harold received word of the activity in the Norman camp, and his military knowledge and experience would tell him that he was likely to be attacked early in the morning. This put him in a quandary: his army was not assembled at anything like full strength; possibly the marching levies were not coming in as quickly as he had anticipated; maybe that on arrival they were more exhausted than he expected; some contingents may have broken their word and gone home instead of marching to battle. Earls Edwin and Morcar from the north had promised contingents, but were slow to move and took no part in the fight at Hastings. He must make up his mind quickly, and we can be sure he did so. Senlac Hill, which his advanced troops were holding to cover the concentration of his force, must now become his main position. He must fight a defensive battle and hope that enough levies would arrive in sufficient time to withstand William's assault and enable him to make a successful counter-attack before dark.

This is what I think happened.

In a matter of a few hours William had seized the initiative—to use modern military parlance. Now *he* was setting the pace. With his army fresh and concentrated he was about to attack an English army still in process of deployment and in a very tired, if not exhausted, condition.

✝ BATTLE—14th OCTOBER 1066

The old chroniclers—none of them eye-witnesses—have given us descriptions of many romantic incidents about this battle—how William's half-brother, Odo, Bishop of Bayeux, held Mass for the whole Norman force before leaving Hastings and how the Duke made an impassioned speech to his army immediately before battle. There may be some truth in these stories, and many others, but the magnitude of the task of one man conducting Mass, and another addressing some nine thousand men, without a public address system, makes one somewhat sceptical of these tales. One of the Norman chroniclers tells us that the Duke's men spent the night in prayer and the English in feasting and revelry—very unlikely ways of spending the last few hours before a fight of such importance. After their exhausting march from London Harold's men would be dog-tired, and, even if they had possessed the necessary supplies of food and drink, would hardly be likely to spend a bleak autumn night in the open in that way, when there was so much to be done.

We can dismiss most of these flowery stories as being typical of the 'chronicler's licence' prevailing in those times. My reconstruction of the battle which follows is based on the few known facts, and what I believe to be a reasonable and likely—although not always certain—course of events.

As indicated earlier, I believe that by about midnight on 13–14th October, possibly considerably earlier, the two

E

sides had a fairly good idea of what was afoot in the opposing camp. I cannot accept the view of some historians that the battle of Hastings was a chance affair, in which Harold was surprised to find the Normans approaching his position when they did, and the Duke equally surprised to find the English barring his path on Senlac Hill. It seems inconceivable to me that two rival armies, no more than six miles apart, and each comprising several thousand men, should be ignorant of the undisguised activities of each other.

Before proceeding with the story we must consider the terrain of the battle area as it was in 1066. Reference should be made to Maps III and IV, printed on pages 58, 59, and on endpapers, and show the area as it is today and as I believe it was nine hundred years ago. To the north of the present village of Battle was the thick forest area of the Weald from which Harold's men debouched as they dribbled in to Senlac Hill. The old Roman road from Hastings leading north-west to the battle area undoubtedly still existed at that time, but was almost certainly ill kept. The present road has a curve to the east near the abbey; but I think there can be no doubt that it ran straight (that is through, or very near to, the abbey site as indicated on Map III) in 1066. It will also be noted from the map that the flanks of the Senlac position are admirably protected by sloping ground which provides a considerable hindrance, if not an obstacle, to horsemen. The line of the Senlac Brook, between the English position and Norman line of deployment, was probably boggy, as were several other low-lying areas. Finally the slope up to the English position, although a comparatively gentle one, would tire the heavily laden, and probably not too fit, mounts of the Norman knights.

In short, Harold's army occupied a very strong position, which could only be attacked by cavalry frontally and then over boggy ground and uphill.

As a general rule medieval armies had little liking for night operations. Their idea of a battle was one which started soon after an early breakfast and finished in time for the survivors to have a late supper. By our time sunrise in mid October is about 6.20 a.m., and one would suppose, therefore, that the Normans would start their march at about that time or a little earlier. By the standards of modern march formations the column would be about three or four miles long; but, if I am correct in supposing that William had a good inkling of the whereabouts and dispositions of the English, he probably moved with his army 'closed up' or 'double banked'. In that case his force would extend to half, or perhaps one-third, of that distance from front to rear, and could be deployed for action comparatively quickly.

Meanwhile Harold's men had been working all night to strengthen the position on Senlac Hill. I think it is reasonable to assume that he had spies and mounted scouts out watching the Norman camp, and that some time about 7 a.m. he would get word that the Duke was on the move. Thereafter he would get further reports of the progress and direction of the march. Similarly William's mounted patrols, well out in front of his main body, would locate the English army and confirm the Duke's previous information as to its position.

By about 8 a.m. the leading men of the Norman main body would have reached Blackhorse Hill, and the column or columns very likely halted while William made a

reconnaissance and plan, and issued his orders. Some
authorities think that he may have done his reconnaissance
the previous evening, when enough of Harold's men were
on the spot to disclose the extent of the English position. I
think this is just conceivable, but very unlikely. He may,
however, have occupied Telham Hill with a strong detachment the previous evening. We can do no more than
guess, and my guess is that the Duke made his reconnaissance at about 8.15 a.m. from Telham Hill, near the spot
marked W.R. on Maps III and IV. I cannot think of any
other place. It is true that today, owing to trees and a few
modern buildings, the English position is not clearly visible,
but I believe much of it was in 1066. By about 8.45 a.m.
William was probably back at the head of his main body
issuing orders.

The next phase was the deployment of the Norman army
in battle array. The eventual line taken up was of conven-
tional pattern—namely parallel to, and opposite, the
English position—and was approximately as shown on the
map. We have no details as to how the deployment was
carried out. Colonel Burne suggested that the Duke
marched his men up the road to the kink (marked D on the
map) about 300 yards west of Starr's Green, and then moved
due west across country on to the line of deployment. This
may have been the way it was done; but if the Norman
army was already well closed up, and moving in more than
one column, it is likely that the troops left the road a mile
or so before reaching Starr's Green. This is something we
shall never know for certain.[1]

[1] The two possible methods of deployment have been marked on
Map III.

Whatever method was adopted it seems that the army deployed in three columns or divisions:

1. *Left:* Mainly Bretons, with the Breton Count Alan Fergant in command.
2. *Centre:* Normans, led by the Duke.
3. *Right:* French and Flemings, with Eustace of Boulogne and the Norman Baron Roger of Montgomery.

In each column there were three echelons: in front archers; behind them foot-soldiers, and in the rear the mounted mailed knights. Although each had a quota of knights it seems likely that the centre column under William had more than the other two.

I do not think the deployment is likely to have been completed before 9.30 or even 10 a.m. This is later than some historians give for the start of the battle; but I think there is a tendency to underestimate the time it would take William's men to march six or seven miles, carry out the necessary reconnaissance, issue orders, shake out into the appropriate three columns and move up to the 'Start Line'. I also find some difficulty in visualizing how the battle continued into the late afternoon if it began as early as some authorities believe.

If details of the Norman deployment are lacking, those of the English dispositions are very much more so. But I do not find it difficult to give the frontage with some confidence. I think that with this almost ideal defensive position for an eleventh-century infantry army, Harold would certainly extend his flanks so as to get the maximum protection from the rising ground at both ends, which, if not a complete obstacle to cavalry, would be a very great hindrance. I think that all the same he would probably protect

his flanks by positioning special bodies of troops for the
purpose.

When, however, we come to the details of the English
dispositions the problem becomes more difficult—in fact
entirely a matter of reasonable surmise. Apart from some
reinforcement for the 'shield wall' I do not believe that
Harold constructed any very elaborate 'palisade' or
extensive earthworks. Firstly he did not have time to do so,
and secondly his aim would be to get to grips with the
Norman horsemen, not to keep them at arm's length. His
only chance of winning the battle was to hack them to
pieces at close quarters and inflict such losses on them as to
make a successful counter-attack, with infantry, a practical
proposition.

I think it likely that the front line was composed of
housecarls, thegns and such of the better equipped and
more reliable shire levies as had arrived. The bulk of the
levies would be in rear, ready to assault any Normans—
horse or foot—who broke through the 'shield wall', and fill
any gaps which might occur in the position.

We do not know with certainty how the command was
divided, but obviously the King commanded the centre in
addition to being the over-all commander. It is reasonable
to think that his brothers—Gurth and Leofwine—were on
either flank, although there is some evidence that they
remained with Harold. The exact position of the King's
command post, distinguished by his two banners—the
Royal Standard of Wessex and his personal one, 'the
Fighting Man'—is known. It was here that Harold died,
and the high altar of the abbey erected by William to
commemorate his victory marks the spot.

My view is that the battle of Hastings began between 9.30

a.m. and 10 a.m. on 14th October 1066, by which time the opposing armies were facing each other 700 to 1,000 yards apart.

It is interesting to speculate on the reactions of the two sides at that moment. Except for Harold and a few of his close associates the English troops had never seen a mounted array of the size or kind of the Norman contingent of knights. This may well have given the shire levies and some of the thegns a shock, but the professional housecarls would not be greatly impressed. They had probably heard stories of continental knights who practised some novel trick of fighting from the backs of horses, but when the test came they were fairly confident they could deal with this innovation. The Duke's men were probably impressed by the obvious strength of the position and the formidable appearance of the housecarls in the front line; but, nevertheless, confident in their superior skill and armour to win the day.

Before describing the actual fighting it is well to emphasize two points which are apt to be lost sight of by those who have experienced twentieth-century warfare. The first concerns the knights' mounts. They were not the robust animals of sixteen hands or more to be seen today at English sporting events or ridden by our own Household Cavalry. In 1066 the heavily armoured knight had not yet emerged, and the heavier type of animal to carry him had not been developed. William's cavalrymen were mounted on what today would be classed as ponies: this is confirmed by the Bayeux Tapestry, which generally shows the horses to be very small in comparison with the riders and men on foot. Moreover, the idea of a wild charge by massed horsemen—as depicted in some of the more fanciful pictures of

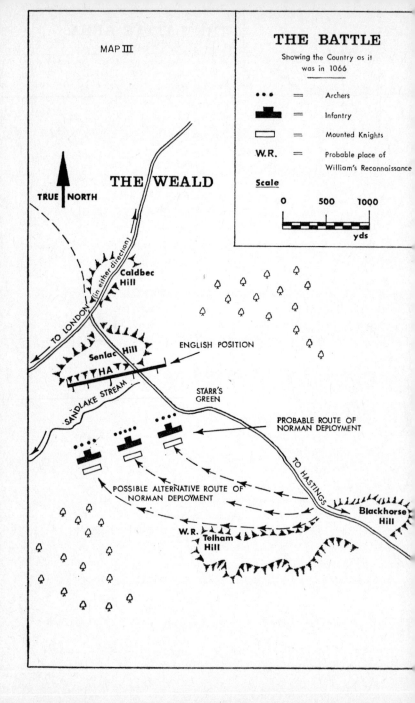

MAP III

THE BATTLE
Showing the Country as it was in 1066

Archers
Infantry
Mounted Knights
W.R. = Probable place of William's Reconnaissance

Scale
0   500   1000
yds

THE WEALD

TRUE NORTH

Caldbec Hill

TO LONDON (in either direction)

Senlac Hill

ENGLISH POSITION

HA

SANDLAKE STREAM

STARR'S GREEN

PROBABLE ROUTE OF NORMAN DEPLOYMENT

POSSIBLE ALTERNATIVE ROUTE OF NORMAN DEPLOYMENT

TO HASTINGS

Blackhorse Hill

W.R.

Telham Hill

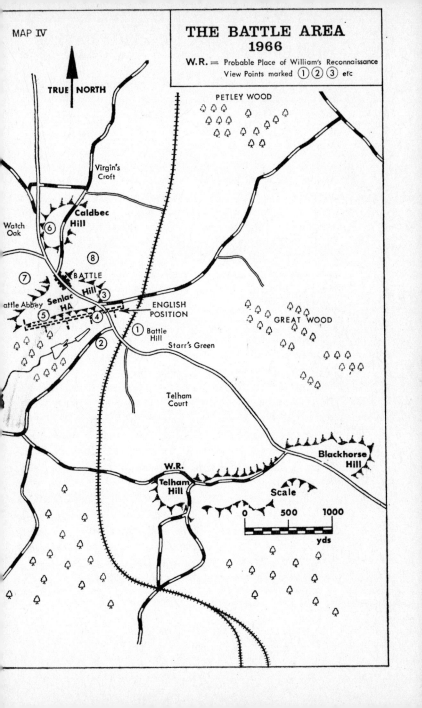

Waterloo and the Charge of the Light Brigade—must be ruled out. I see them moving *uphill*, sometimes at a walk, sometimes at a sedate trot, perhaps at a canter for the last few yards in an attempt to prod a way with their spears through a weak spot in the English position.

The second point to remember is that, except for the arrows of the archers, and any missiles actually thrown or slung, all fighting was hand to hand. I do not think the range of the small bows used by the Normans was more than 150 yards at the most, and consequently there was no danger to life and limb if the opposing ranks were more than that distance apart. The picture of anything like retreating troops being mown down by machine-gun fire, or shelled in their forming-up positions, was totally absent on a medieval battlefield. The opposing ranks were more like the crowds on the pavements on either side of a very wide road, gathered to watch some procession go past.

As I have indicated, the Norman advance probably began between 9.30 and 10 a.m. When the archers got to within range of the English position the whole force halted, while the bowmen delivered a series of low-angle volleys at the defenders. This it was hoped would cause heavy losses and great confusion among Harold's men, who would then be assaulted by the infantry in the hope that gaps would be made in the line through which the mounted men could penetrate to give the *coup de grâce*.

That I feel sure was the tactical plan; but it did not work well. The arrows of the archers did not cause the losses and confusion that had been expected, and William's infantry were beaten back. It is doubtful if any serious attack by the cavalry was made during the initial assault, but some of the more impetuous knights may have tried to make an

impression on the 'shield wall' when they saw the failure of
the infantry. On their right and centre the Norman withdrawal was orderly; but on the left the Bretons dashed down
the hill in headlong flight. This proved too much for Harold's
men on that (the English right) flank, who left their defensive
position and pursued them into the valley. This gave
William a chance partially to retrieve an ugly situation. He
immediately wheeled some of the cavalry of his centre
column to the left, where they attacked the pursuing
English in flank, causing very heavy losses. As we shall see,
this episode was to have very important results.

There now came one of those pauses which in all ages,
and all kinds of fighting, usually follow an unsuccessful
assault. This pause was probably longer than usual,
because the Norman archers could not replenish their
arrows from those fired by the enemy, as was customary in
continental warfare at that time. The English had no
archers, or very few. In consequence it is believed that the
Normans had to bring up fresh supplies of ammunition in
country carts. William now had to reorganize his battered
troops and do some quick thinking for his next move.
Harold had to patch up his disorganized right flank, and no
doubt issue a warning to his troops as to what happens when
ill discipline results in a premature pursuit. All this time
more levies were arriving to increase the strength of the
English host, a fact which would not have escaped William's
notice, making him realize that any delay in continuing the
battle decreased his chance of success.

Having completed a quick reorganization of his army and
issued further orders, William embarked on his second
attack. It is difficult to say when this took place, but not
before noon and probably later in the early afternoon. This

attack seems to have met with more success than the first, and some gaps were made in the English line. The mounted men appear to have played a more important part in this assault than in the earlier one. Losses were very heavy on both sides, but in spite of all their efforts the Normans were unable to bring about the disintegration of their foe which they had expected, and it looked as if this attack was to peter out like the first.

It was at this stage that the Duke is supposed to have initiated a feigned flight on part of the front. Exactly where this occurred is not certain, but it is clear that the English, thinking the attackers had panicked, again left their defensive positions in pursuit. When they were nearing the bottom of the hill the Duke, repeating his previous tactics, attacked them in flank with a body of horsemen from another part of the front. Few of the English involved in this incident escaped.[1]

This second example of the power of cavalry must have shaken the English, and at this stage—probably about mid afternoon—the Duke decided that one more determined attack would achieve victory. Time was getting short (by our time sunset was about 5 p.m.) and he resolved on an all-out effort by the cavalry, supported by the archers. It seems probable that by then the English line had been considerably contracted. We know that their right flank had suffered an early setback and it may be that the second debacle, described above, was on the other flank. If in fact the position had been contracted it would enable the Norman knights to assault on the flanks, as the steeper

---

[1] Many historians are sceptical about the feigned nature of this retreat; but as far as results are concerned it matters little whether it was genuine or feigned. The matter is discussed in greater detail in the next chapter.

ground on the original flanks would no longer afford the same protection.

This final attack, which appears to have gone on for some time, consisted of a series of determined mounted assaults covered by volleys of arrows. Gradually the English were worn down, and one can easily imagine the further contraction of the position round the King and his standards. At some stage in this final phase the archers were ordered to use high-angle fire—almost certainly directed at the area occupied by Harold. The situation got worse and worse for the English. The King's two brothers—Gurth and Leofwine —had both fallen and morale would be at a low ebb. Some of the thegns, and probably many of the shire levies, had decamped or were on the point of doing so. Only the gallant housecarls fought on without thought of the consequences.

Eventually Harold was hit in the eye by one of the high-angle arrows. The news soon spread and the process of disintegration was accelerated. But the surviving housecarls still continued to fight on round their wounded King. The last act in the drama was when a party of knights penetrated the last line of defence and killed the wounded Harold.

And so the Saxon line of English kings came to an end. In a matter of a few hours a single conflict, in which at the most twenty thousand were engaged, changed the history of England and the story of a substantial part of the rest of the world.

It is not difficult to imagine the scene of carnage on Senlac Hill on that October evening nine hundred years ago. On the crest, where the Saxon position had been, the dead and dying—men and horses—would be lying literally in heaps. The walking wounded—some with slight injuries, others only just able to crawl along—would, in the case of the Normans, be mingled with the dead and dying on the southern slopes of Senlac and in the valley: the English would be making their way to sanctuary in the woods to the north. As depicted in the Bayeux Tapestry, the Norman survivors were busy removing the mail, headgear and any other valuable equipment or clothing from the dead. It was a scene no less frightful than the Somme, Passchendaele or the Falaise pocket of our times.

Any attempt to estimate casualties must be little more than guesswork. The old chroniclers had little idea of figures, and whenever they attempted to assess numbers they were nearly always wildly wrong. More recent writers are little better: at least one has given fifty thousand as the strength of William's army, and the English even more.

Hastings was, however, a desperate battle and the losses were heavy on both sides. Several authorities give the Norman losses as about one-quarter of the whole force, namely two thousand or slightly more. That presumably is the figure for the killed and mortally wounded, and it seems a likely one as a rough estimate.

The English casualties were probably much heavier, especially among the *élite* of the army—the leaders and the housecarls. The King and his two brothers were killed, and of the top leaders only two are said to have escaped— Esegar the Staller and Leofric, Abbot of Bourne, and they were both seriously wounded. A high proportion of the thegns of southern England also perished on this day.

The extent to which the Normans exploited their success by pursuit is obscure. Medieval horsemen, as a general rule, eschewed warlike operations by night. The survivors of the

English army took refuge in the forbidding forest to the north, and this would be particularly unsuitable for cavalry, even by day. Although some accounts indicate that William ordered an 'implacable pursuit' I doubt if this extended deep into the Weald, or was carried out by more than a small proportion of his mounted men.

I think the so-called pursuit was probably a local affair confined to cutting down stragglers and wounded in the narrow belt of comparatively open country between Senlac Hill and the Weald. Small parties of impetuous knights may have penetrated the forest, but I suspect that the majority found the exertions of the battle enough for one day. Some accounts have made a great deal of the misfortunes of some knights who plunged into a deep ravine (later known as the 'Malfosse'), where they were set upon by some survivors of Harold's men. This has been magnified into a major incident; but I do not see it that way: I think it more likely that it was a comparatively trivial incident involving a small party of over-eager knights in the half-light.[1] But it made a good story for the chroniclers.

[1] This matter is of some historical interest and is more fully dealt with in the next chapter under the heading 'The Malfosse'.

V

Comment on Operations

See Maps II, III and IV

In the last chapter an attempt has been made to reconstruct the battle by supplementing the meagre known facts with reasonable assumptions. In order not to disturb the narrative, controversial matters were not discussed in detail, except in a few instances where this was considered necessary for a proper understanding of the story. The purpose of this chapter is to discuss in greater detail some of the interesting controversial points which inevitably arise.

'CONTRARY WINDS'

As explained in Chapter III, there is evidence that William of Normandy was ready for the invasion of England by the first half of August 1066. That would be a very suitable time of year for an enterprise of this kind. He had no reason to believe that he could win the crown of England by a single battle. It was more likely that he would have to fight a campaign lasting some weeks, possibly months. He would therefore want a good period of suitable campaigning weather. As it was he took a considerable risk in landing as late as the end of September and not starting active operations until mid October. He might well have been caught by severe winter conditions with the campaign undecided.

There must therefore have been a good reason for the delay. This has always been attributed to 'contrary winds' in the Channel, an explanation which, as far as I know, has never been seriously disputed. I have little knowledge of sailing, or meteorology; but the very first time I read of William's delay owing to 'contrary winds' I had a feeling that it might not be the true reason. Some years later, when I came to study the Norman invasion more closely, I looked for a possible alternative reason, and took steps to find out something about weather conditions in the English Channel in August and September.

There *is* a possible alternative reason. If it could be shown that William was aware of the plans of Harald of Norway for *his* invasion of England and bid for the English crown—particularly if he knew the approximate time of his proposed landing—then we have a sufficient reason for William's delay. It would obviously be to his advantage to time his landing when Harold of England was in the north battling against another formidable enemy. Unfortunately there is no likelihood of ever discovering with certainty if William's timing of events was governed by this factor. Communications between Norway and Normandy would be difficult, and in time more a matter of weeks than of days. It is, however, possible that the Norwegian king had some long-term plan for landing at a particular time and that William knew of this, and had sufficient faith in it to base his own plans on its implementation. The Norwegian king's intentions seem to have been widely known, and there are good grounds for assuming that Harold expected an invasion from that direction.

F

Before examining the technical aspect of weather conditions in the Channel it will be as well to state in greater detail the events during the weeks preceding William's embarkation. The ships to convey the army to England were constructed and collected at a number of ports along the Normandy coast. It is believed that the original plan was to assemble the whole fleet at the mouth of the small River Dives (some twenty miles west of the mouth of the Seine), and that this had been done by early August. After waiting there for a favourable wind for about a month a violent storm broke from the west, forcing the fleet up the cost in a north-easterly direction. The ships then anchored at the mouth of the Somme off St Valéry-sur-Somme. No doubt the storm caused some losses and damage. That seems a likely story. Some accounts state that William's ships were attacked by the English fleet about the same time; but I know of no reliable evidence for this, and it seems unlikely.

In the course of probing the 'contrary winds' theory I have discussed weather conditions in the Channel with a number of people with knowledge of the subject. Some are yachtsmen with practical experience of sailing in those waters, others being expert meteorologists. Among the latter was the well-known authority on the history of climate, Mr H. H. Lamb, of the Meteorological Office at Bracknell in Berkshire.[1] I will not attempt to give details, or go into the technicalities involved, but confine my remarks to a summary of the salient facts, and my conclusions.

The English climate, as we know well, is very difficult to predict, and in late summer and autumn it is particularly so. The wind in the Channel may blow in almost any direction, although west and north-west are perhaps the most usual,

[1] Mr Lamb is the author of the book *The English Climate*.

and storms are likely. It is a characteristic—although by no means an invariable rule—that long spells of similar wind may occur. This fits in with the story, passed down by the old chroniclers, of a violent storm from the west which drove the Duke's ships up the coast and 'contrary winds' blowing from mid August to nearly the end of September. It must also be borne in mind that William was not in a position to take advantage of a snap chance. His cosmopolitan army was not very well disciplined and could not embark with its horses at very short notice. The indication had to be that a favourable wind would last for some days, and no doubt the local weather experts—who in all ages are to be found in coastal areas—gave him good advice.

An interesting point to note is that a contrary wind for the Duke would very likely be a favourable one for the Norwegians. East or north-east would have suited the latter admirably. If William was aware of Harald of Norway's intention, and he very likely was, the persistent 'contrary winds' would tend to confirm his belief that Hardrada's invasion would in fact take place. William's belief in this may well account for his determination to carry through his plan. Storm, 'contrary winds', disaffection in his army— none of these seem to have damped his resolve, and this could be because he knew that, if he delayed for any considerable time, he would be unlikely to get such a favourable opportunity again. Whoever won the battle in the north would be a weakened opponent.

The 'contrary winds' *cum* 'Harald of Norway' discussion is a very interesting one, but one which cannot be decided with any degree of certainty. I think a very likely story is that the storm *did* take place and that it damaged William's ships much more than most historians have believed. If this is so it may have been a major factor in delaying the expedition, and the period of 'contrary winds' may have been less, perhaps a lot less, than six weeks. Moreover, it is more than probable that William, through his spies in England, knew that the vigil of the shire levies and English fleet could not, for reasons of supply, go on beyond the late summer.

The delay of the invasion until the end of September could, therefore, have been due to a combination of circumstances—the storm, the English vigil on the coast, 'contrary winds' and the knowledge that delay would be an advantage if it resulted in the landing coinciding with one from Norway. The fact that the Duke landed three days after the Stamford Bridge battle—an almost perfect piece of timing —could not, I feel, have been a complete fluke.

STRATEGY AND TACTICS

Neither the old chroniclers nor later writers have given much attention to the strategy of the events of 1066—that is, the various preliminary moves before the battle, which resulted in the Normans fighting under very much better conditions than the English. Almost without exception they have concentrated on the battle itself and attributed William's victory to the superior quality and equipment of his troops, and particularly to his possession of a large force of cavalry and some archers. This neglect of strategy is largely due to the fact that most of the writers—ancient and modern—were scholars or professional historians without any special knowledge of military affairs.

The late Lieutenant-Colonel A. H. Burne, mentioned earlier in this book, is one of the few writers who deal with the strategic aspect, and he does so in a manner which I find surprising.[1] He writes in somewhat scathing terms about William's dilatoriness, and lack of initiative, in remaining stationary for sixteen days at Hastings, and implies his approval of Harold's vigorous action and eagerness to join battle with the Norman invaders. He gives the impression that their superior efficiency and armament won the day for the Normans *in spite of* the Duke's dithering.

My own view is quite different. I agree that the mobility and shock action of the Norman knights, the effective fire of the archers, and the generally better training of the Duke's men, gave them a considerable battlefield advantage over the English—who except for the housecarls were amateur soldiers. On the other hand I feel that William's strategy was very nearly faultless, although this may have been due partly to good fortune rather than design. The same cannot be said of Harold's strategy. In my opinion the strategic factor played at least an equal part with the battlefield tactics in bringing about the Duke's victory and the King's defeat. The battle was a close-run affair, and if Harold could have brought more men in better condition to Senlac Hill the victory might well have been his. If I am correct in this view the preliminary strategic moves merit much closer attention than they have been accorded by most writers.

The purpose of strategy, as applied to medieval warfare, was to bring the largest possible force to the appropriate battlefield in the best fighting condition. It is interesting to examine the extent to which the two sides fulfilled these conditions.

The size of William's force was probably governed by the amount of suitable shipping available. To collect or

[1] See *The Battlefields of England*, by Lieutenant-Colonel Alfred H. Burne, D.S.O. (1950), Chapter III.

construct, load, navigate to the English coast and unload a
fleet of some 700 ships, carrying about 11,000 men and 3,600
horses, was no mean feat. We have no reason to believe that
the Duke could have brought more men. Once he had
landed, the numbers he deployed on the battlefield would
depend on the avoidance of sickness among men and
animals, and the elimination of wasteful detachments and
men employed on duties not directly connected with fighting. It is believed that small garrisons were left at Pevensey
and Hastings; but there is no reason to believe that the Duke
did not assemble the largest possible force for the battle.

We know little of what went on in the Hastings area
during the sixteen days between the Norman landing and
the battle. Undoubtedly supplies for men and animals were
collected and the camp at Hastings was fortified against an
attack of the kind delivered by Harold at Stamford Bridge
and which he very likely intended delivering against
William. If this happened it is only reasonable to suppose
that the Duke's plan was to let the English batter themselves to exhaustion against the defences and then launch
his mounted knights in a decisive counter-attack. But some
time during 13th October it seems that William received
word that Harold was concentrating his forces on or near
Senlac Hill. He decided to attack him before his concentration was complete and, as we know, the outcome was the
successful battle on the following day.

There seems little to find fault with in this strategy. If we
concede that William also timed his landing to coincide
with that of Harald of Norway—a doubtful point, but a
possibility—we must surely agree that William of Normandy was a strategist of the first order, comparable with
Field Marshal Lord Montgomery, who conducted operations

in the reverse direction nearly nine centuries later. He also had the reputation of being strategically cautious—a man who, very wisely, liked to make victory as certain as possible—but who acted vigorously and boldly once battle had been joined.

There is one more point worth mentioning before we leave the Duke. There is evidence that he had been warned that if he did not take the initiative Harold would assemble an army of overwhelming strength in London. It may be that he was preparing to move north, probably on the capital, when he got news that the English army was about to assemble at Senlac.

We can now turn to Harold. There can be nothing but approval for the prompt manner in which he left York for the south as soon as he heard of the Norman landing. He also seems to have acted with vigour in alerting the shire levies of the south midlands, South and East Anglia, and in initiating the assembly of an army in London. Thereafter his action was less commendable. For some reason, which we do not know with certainty, he decided to carry out a fifty-eight-mile march to Senlac Hill before his army had completed its concentration in London. The cause may have been either a desire to free southern England from William's 'fire and sword' policy as soon as possible or a wrong interpretation of William's intentions; but it was more likely due to an impetuous nature accentuated by his recent resounding victory at Stamford Bridge. The result was fatal: he was caught with a tired army, only a fraction of the size it might have been, in a hastily prepared position. Had he delayed a few days he might have fought the battle on the same ground—or elsewhere, we cannot be sure—but with a concentrated army, less fatigued and at full strength.

I do not think these facts can be disputed, and, if accepted, it is evident that at the battle of Hastings in 1066 the Normans fought under very much more favourable conditions than the English. In view of the closeness of the actual fight it is not too much to say that the superior strategy of the Normans may well have decided the issue, with all its fateful consequences.

THE ENGLISH POSITION ON SENLAC HILL

The nature and extent of the English position on Senlac Hill must be a matter for speculation; but, as so many of the events of that time are no more than speculation, there is no reason why we should not probe the problem and try to get some idea of how Harold's men were deployed and protected.

The first item for investigation is the extent of the position: where was the front line? We know with certainty that the site of the abbey was roughly the centre of the position. It was here that Harold's two standards were placed; this was his command post and the spot where he died. In the accounts of the battle there is no hint that the Norman knights made any attempt to get round the flanks of the position, except perhaps in the final stages just before the King's death. The deduction from this is that the position extended on both flanks to the precipitous ground —called the 'ravines' in some accounts—which acted as a protection against a cavalry assault. I therefore think that the position as given on Map III is the most likely. The various authorities differ widely in this matter, Freeman and George giving much longer frontages, and Oman and Saltzmann much shorter. It is not, however, a matter of great moment. We know the approximate centre of the line; but we do not

PLATE 3. A SECTION OF THE BAYEUX TAPESTRY

These illustrations show many of the weapons used in the battle. The second figure from the left is an English housecarl with his bill and what appears to be a round shield with many arrows sticking into it. He is being attacked by a Norman knight (apparently jerked out of his

ANT CVM hAROLDO :.

HAROLD'S MEN ARE KILLED

saddle) armed with a sword and carrying a kite-shaped shield. On the right is an unarmed and seemingly wounded shire levy, and on the extreme right is part of a mounted Norman carrying a spear. The lower border shows Norman archers in action.

know enough about the other details of the battle to make the exact location of the flanks a matter of the first importance.

We can now consider the question of what defences, if any, Harold was able to construct in the limited time at his disposal. It seems that the traditional English system of defence in a set-piece battle was the 'shield wall', the men standing shoulder to shoulder holding their kite-shaped (or sometimes round) shields so as to protect them from the neck downwards to just above the knee: that is, with the pointed end about two feet from the ground. This is how the English are shown in the Bayeux Tapestry. I, however, find it hard to believe that the shields were invariably used in this way. The traditional weapon of the English was the bill, which was a two-handed weapon. I cannot see that a man using such a weapon could also hold a large shield. Even if it was strapped to his body it would be a very considerable hindrance to the use of the bill. It has been suggested that the English fought in small teams, some of each team providing the shield wall and others using their weapons; but I doubt this and can find no evidence to support it. My own view is that the shield wall often consisted of shields propped up in some way or stuck into the ground. This would enable the defenders to crouch behind them when under fire from arrows or other missiles, but leave them free to use their weapons when the enemy came within striking distance. If I am correct in this opinion it would explain why most of the English shields were pointed at the lower end,[1] as this would make them easier to stick into the ground; although it does not explain why the shields of the mounted Norman knights were of similar pattern.

[1] Some English shields were round. One such is shown in the Bayeux Tapestry; but the majority were of the kite-shaped variety.

The historian Freeman, in *The Norman Conquest*, claims that the English built a 'palisade' along their entire front, basing his statement on indifferently rhymed verse in Wace's *Chronicle*, written ninety years after the battle. I reject the story of an elaborately prepared defensive position. I do not believe that Harold had time for such work, and there is no suggestion of anything of the kind in the Bayeux Tapestry. This was designed under Norman direction, and those responsible would have been only too eager to illustrate the formidable nature of the English defences had any existed. I believe that the traditional shield wall was the basis of the defence. The shields may have been stuck in the ground or carried; I would favour the former were it not for the fact that they are shown as being carried in the Tapestry. I do not think that any extensive works were constructed; but they may have collected some timber from the forest and a few boulders or other local material to reinforce the shield wall.

Another suggestion is that Senlac Hill had been the scene of an older battle—possibly one of Alfred's against the Danes—and that defensive earthworks constructed at that time were used by Harold's men to augment the shield wall. This is a possible explanation, the word 'palisade' being wrongly used to describe these old entrenchments. In view of the extensive building and agriculture which have taken place over the centuries it is not surprising that there are no signs of these earthworks today.

THE MANNER OF THE FIGHTING

It is interesting to try to depict what a medieval battle was really like. Those with recent experience know that a modern battle is not always as the artists show it. In the pictures men and horses, and later machines, show an eagerness to advance which is not always apparent on the battlefield. On the canvas everything is tidier than it is in practice—the men are clean and well turned out, they maintain excellent formation, the horses are sleek and well groomed and display little apprehension at what is happening.

It is the same with the Bayeux Tapestry—the only worth-while pictorial record we have of Hastings or any other battle of that era. The knights are immaculately turned out and their mounts eager to press on and see what it is like to receive a thrust from an English spear, or a blow from a bill. Similarly the English infantry appear to be quite unperturbed by the array of horsemen charging them. I think it must have been very different on the field on the day.

The first thing to realize is that there was little or no attempt at concealment from view and no need to seek protection from fire. The two armies assembled in the open in full view of each other.

The English were no doubt in position when the Norman host made its appearance. The King and other leaders were very likely mounted at this stage, and riding up and down the line making adjustments and encouraging their men. In rear there was probably much activity as batches of shire levies continued to arrive and were assigned to their battle positions.

It is not fanciful to suppose that the Norman line of deployment was indicated by mounted 'markers', very much the same as is done today on a big ceremonial occasion—except that now the markers are usually on foot. There would be much shouting of orders and general bustle before the Duke was satisfied. Finally he would ride along the line to make quite sure all was well, and perhaps give some final instructions to some of his subordinate leaders. The word to advance would then be given—the archers leading, followed by the bulk of the infantry, and then the mounted knights in rear.

At first the pace would be slow; after one or two hundred yards it would quicken, but never become very fast. There was no need for hurry until they came within range of the primitive English missiles—from slings, or spears and the like thrown by hand. When the archers got within effective range—probably about a hundred yards or less—the whole army would halt. By this time the two arrays were within shouting distance of each other, and there would almost certainly be an exchange of uncomplimentary remarks— the English probably the more vocal, taunting the enemy to stop shooting his stupid arrows and come and fight it out at close quarters.

When the archers had fired the amount of ammunition prescribed by the Duke, the infantry would pass through them, quickening their pace considerably when they came within range of the English missiles. Hand-to-hand fighting would take place. Meanwhile the knights would move forward a little, seeking eagerly for a gap in the defenders' line which would enable them to enter the position. Some, perhaps over-eager, would advance to what they thought looked like a weak spot and, spurring their reluctant mounts forward, try to prod a way through with their spears. But, as we know, this first assault did not go well. In the centre and right an orderly withdrawal was carried out —probably not as far as the original line of deployment, but some way down the hill. On the left, however, the Bretons' withdrawal became a headlong flight, in which they were pursued by the excited English opposite them.

This gave the Duke a chance to get even with his obstinate foe. In an instant he gave the word for a mounted detachment from the centre column to wheel to the left and attack the English in flank. Here again we must not imagine the wild charge, at full gallop, of the picture books. The ground may have been boggy and broken, and the knights were moving obliquely across quite a noticeable slope. They would want to keep together in formation—in the manner of Cromwell's Ironsides nearly six hundred years later. I see the movements being made at a brisk trot, perhaps a collected canter where the going was good or for the last twenty-five or thirty yards.

With the completion of this successful action there would be a considerable pause, with much sorting out on both sides. Harold would have to reorganize his right flank and probably speak sharply to the commander there—if he was still alive—for permitting such an ill-disciplined and premature pursuit. William would be equally curt with the Bretons, and would be busy reorganizing for the next assault.

Later the second attack would be launched. The procedure would be much the same. There would be signs that the English were tiring and their casualties heavy; but still the line held and the Normans were again forced to withdraw without any decisive result.

Another pause—not so long as the previous one perhaps —and then the final, and successful, assault. This followed the same pattern as the two others, but the opportunities for cavalry action were greater. The archers and the infantry assaults had worn the defence down; the English line became contracted, exposing the flanks to attack, and gaps appeared through which the knights were able to penetrate.

That is the manner in which I believe the fighting on Senlac Hill was conducted nine hundred years ago. The battle was not decided by some cunning tactical plan, but by solid close-quarter fighting. The side which had been brought the fresher and fitter to the battlefield, and which possessed modern armament and practised modern technique, won the day.

THE FEIGNED RETREAT

There appear to have been at least two hasty retreats by William's army in this battle—retreats in the nature of flights rather than orderly withdrawals. The first of these took place during the first attack when the Bretons on the left flank gave way. There seems to be no doubt that this was a genuine retreat by troops who had panicked. There was at least one other hasty retreat—in my judgment only one, although some writers give more—and I put this as taking place during the second attack. It seems that it is this retreat which two of the old chroniclers—Guy of Amiens and William of Poitiers—describe as a feint retreat, deliberately contrived to draw the English out of their position so that the mounted men could deal with them in the open.

A number of answers to this question have been expounded over the years, but I think there are only two which bear the mark of probability.

First, that it was a genuine retreat on a part of the front occupied by Normans. The chroniclers—being Normans—would not like to admit this, but as it was one of the most important incidents in the battle they could hardly ignore it altogether. The obvious line to take was that it was a feigned retreat—a master-stroke of tactics. This would be in accordance with the normal practice of the old chroniclers, who were quite capable of a subterfuge of that kind. They would not have the same qualms about reporting the earlier retreat of the non-Norman Bretons.

Second, that it was in fact a feigned retreat, probably organized as a result of the successful outcome of the previous retreat by the Bretons. This explanation is severely criticized by Lieutenant-Colonel A. H. Burne in his account of the battle. His view is that in the conditions of a medieval battle, and without the help of a trained staff, it would be impossible for William to organize a movement of this kind in the heat of an attack. I agree with this opinion as far as it goes, but I see no reason why it should have been improvised in the heat of an attack. As explained in the last chapter, I believe that there was a long pause, of at least an hour, probably much more, between the first and second attacks. If, as might well be the case, the Duke got the idea of a feigned retreat from the genuine one of the Bretons, it seems to me that it would not have been a very difficult matter for him to organize such a manœuvre during this pause in the battle. It is even possible that a trick of this sort had been discussed during the period at Hastings and become an item in the battle 'drill' of the Duke's army. I see no insuperable difficulty to implementing the idea of a feigned withdrawal and I therefore do not accept Lieutenant-Colonel Burne's view that it was an impossible manœuvre.

I find it difficult to choose between these two courses. On the whole I think I favour the first—that there was no feigned retreat, except in the writings of the chroniclers. I would not, however, discredit the story entirely, as I believe such a manœuvre was quite practicable.

'THE MALFOSSE'

According to a number of writers a party of Norman knights, either towards the end of the battle or during the pursuit, came to grief in a hidden ravine, precipice or ditch covered with grass, as it is variously described. This place has become known as the 'Malfosse'; some think because of the owner's name, which might have been 'Mansers', although there is no shred of evidence of this.

The end piece of the Bayeux Tapestry shows some horses without riders and in various attitudes of disaster. Some authorities have pointed to this as the 'Malfosse', but I do not think it is the case. The Tapestry, to my mind, shows clearly that it represents a mounted attack on the Senlac Hill and that the misfortunes of the mounted knights are due to the action of the defending English. We must look elsewhere for the site of the 'Malfosse'. Freeman, in *The Norman Conquest*, published in 1869, places it immediately behind the left flank of the English position. Baring suggests a quite different place, namely some six hundred yards behind the right flank, and in this he is supported by Lieutenant-Colonel Burne.

The fact is we have no idea, or any real pointer to the location of this place, or the true significance of the incident. I feel that it has been magnified out of all proportion to its importance. I think it likely that no more than a dozen, perhaps half a dozen, knights were involved in the affair, probably in the half-light when dealing with English stragglers after the battle. They may have been ambushed and driven into some ravine or ditch. The survivors would tell the tale far and wide and it would not lose in the telling —as has happened so many times with minor incidents in our own two wars. It bears the stamp of the 'old soldier's' story!

VI

The Aftermath and
Consequences of Battle

The aftermath and consequences of the great battle of 14th October 1066 fall into three categories: events immediately following the battle, the completion of the Norman Conquest and the ultimate influence on British and world history. The first of these is of interest but not of great moment; the second is history of the first importance; the last is an interesting mental exercise into what might, or might not, have been the long-term consequences of an English, instead of a Norman, victory at Hastings. I feel that all three are of sufficient interest and importance to justify a brief description and comment. The story of a battle cannot be complete without at least a summary of its consequences. The battle itself was a savage incident, of only a few hours' duration, involving a few thousand men, but its consequences were felt far and wide by countless millions for many generations.

AFTER THE BATTLE

It is a matter of surprise to most people, when they first read the story of the Norman Conquest, that the crown and realm of England could have fallen to the Conqueror as a result of a single battle. That is virtually what happened for, although fighting went on for some years, it was in reality 'mopping-up', bringing the remoter parts of the country into the fold or suppressing some minor uprising; never a really serious threat to William as the King of England.

Had the England of the eleventh century been a nation as we know the term today, this single-battle conquest could not have happened. But Saxon-Danish England was not a nation. The nobility, ecclesiastical dignitaries and gentry (thegns) fought for their possessions—their land, their cattle, their homes, their privileges and prestige. The rest of the country had nothing that would not be just as safe under Norman as under English rule. There was no English patriotism and, as we have seen earlier, there was an influential Norman 'fifth column' already established in the country.

The only people who could have sustained a campaign against the invaders were the leaders, who had everything to lose, but they no longer existed in sufficient numbers. The King and two of his brothers, and most of the leaders resident in the south midlands, East Anglia and the south of England, had fallen at Hastings. The two great earls of the north—Edwin and Morcar—had recently suffered defeat at the hands of the Norwegian king before his own defeat at Stamford Bridge. They seem to have had the impression that they were sufficiently remote from the capital to remain neutral and continue under William in possession of their lands and appointments. Only the citizens of London appear to have been in the frame of mind to defend their city, their possessions and their liberties, and even they soon changed their attitude.

These few sentences explain how it came about that the crown of England, and all that went with it, changed hands as a result of one battle. But the superficial reader of today is not alone in his surprise at this. It appears that the Conqueror himself was in considerable doubt as to whether his victory at Hastings was decisive or merely the first battle of what might be a long campaign.

For the next few weeks his actions were characterized by caution. The accuracy of detail concerning his movements is no more certain than other events based on the old chroniclers; but the following is as near the truth as we can get.

After the battle William remained for some days in the vicinity of Hastings, hoping that the English leaders in London would offer their submission; but a number of things soon happened to dispel the Duke's optimism. A convoy of ships—sent by his wife, Matilda, with reinforcements—was driven off at Romsey by the still hostile English there. News reached him that the Witan, meeting in London, had nominated Edgar Atheling as king—mainly through the influence of the primate, Stigand, and Aldred, Archbishop of York. There was evidence too that the citizens of London were arming and prepared to defend their city.

These tidings seem to have imbued William with a healthy, and perhaps exaggerated, respect for the power of the Witan and inhabitants of London. His first thought was for his communications with the Continent, and with this in mind he marched the bulk of his army along the coast to Dover with a view to seizing the castle there. Dover Castle had been heavily fortified by Harold, and the Duke no doubt expected it to be a difficult nut to crack. In the event the English garrison surrendered without a fight and was quickly replaced by a Norman garrison. This enabled William to receive reinforcements and provisions from Normandy. He then decided to move on London;[1] but finding the approaches to the city well defended he decided for the time being to confine his activities to burning and plundering the southern outskirts.

Meanwhile, with the advance of the formidable Norman army on the capital, many of Edgar's supporters began to have second thoughts. The earls Morcar and Edwin, who had come to London—and remained there so long as William was still at Hastings—withdrew discreetly to their northern fastnesses. It appears that Esager, who had been severely wounded at Hastings, assumed the military command; but gradually the tide turned and more and more of the leaders prepared to give their allegiance to William.

Fearing to risk a direct assault on London the Duke marched westwards and crossed the Thames near Wallingford, some forty-two miles upstream from London and twelve miles south-east of Oxford. One of the first to meet him there was Stigand, the primate, who offered his submission—a quick turn-about from his recent support of Edgar. He was quickly followed by most of the other dignitaries who had assembled in London, including Aldred of York. Finally Edgar Atheling himself came and offered the crown to William.

These offers of submission seem to have been accepted by William with becoming modesty, and those making them were treated with friendship and hospitality at the time—

---

[1] It should be noted that there is no reliable record of the dates of the moves immediately following the battle.

although not in most cases so well later. The Duke had played his hand with considerable skill. He had avoided a battle for London and, when he finally entered the city, he was able to give the impression of doing so at the request of the leaders of the realm, rather than as a conqueror. His apparent over-caution before and after the battle was in reality politico-military strategy of a very high order—a quality which characterized the Conqueror throughout his life.

The Duke was crowned in Westminster Abbey on Christmas Day 1066. The ceremony, which was performed by Aldred, Archbishop of York, was carried out in accordance with the customs of the Saxon kings. During the ceremony an incident took place which was said to have arisen owing to the exceptionally loud responses of the congregation when asked if they accepted William as their king. The Norman soldiers on guard outside the abbey thought that a popular rising was taking place, and began killing the citizens and burning the nearby houses. But the ceremony was duly completed.

Thus William the Bastard, Duke of Normandy, formally became William I of England, the Conqueror.

COMPLETION OF THE NORMAN CONQUEST

It seems that following the incidents at his coronation the new King did not feel entirely secure in the heart of London and withdrew for a time to Barking, where he received the submission and homage of many more English leaders.

During the period which followed he behaved with

remarkable restraint and showed a desire, at least out-
wardly, to placate his new subjects and do his best to fuse
Normans and English. He confirmed the Londoners in
many of their privileges, as he did Edgar Atheling in the
title of Earl of Oxford which had been conferred on him by
Harold. His army was highly disciplined, and on the whole
a rough justice was enforced in all parts of the country under
William's effective jurisdiction. On the other hand he was
implacable against those who had fought for Harold at
Hastings. The late King's estates were confiscated, as were
those of the whole Godwin family, and many others known
to have actively supported the Saxons whom he considered
had usurped the throne.

In May 1067 William considered his position sufficiently
secure to justify his return to Normandy for a spell; but he
took with him—nominally as part of his retinue, in reality
as hostages—many of the English nobles and prelates,
including Edgar Atheling, Archbishop Stigand, earls Edwin
and Morcar and many others. During his absence the
country was governed by his half-brother—Odo, Bishop of
Bayeux—and William Fitz-Osborne. These two, particularly the latter, seemed to have ruled with a harshness
which was not, as yet, evident in the Conqueror himself
and very soon the discontent of the English began to show
itself in open rebellion. The people of Kent, helped by
Eustace, Count of Boulogne, made an unsuccessful attempt to seize Dover Castle. Edric the Forester joined with
the Welsh, and others in many parts of England, to resist
Norman rule.

On hearing of these events William returned to England
and at once began a campaign to consolidate his new kingdom. Following a successful campaign in the south-west it

could be said that by the end of 1068 he was master of southern England; but in the north, although he was acknowledged as king, his rule, as yet, was not effective. In 1069 the two northern earls—Edwin of Mercia and Morcar of Northumbria—rebelled; being pardoned by William they rebelled again, this time with the help of a Scandinavian invasion under the sons of the Danish king, and assistance from the Welsh. For this the north of England was to pay a heavy price. William's campaign of vengeance virtually reduced the country between York and Durham to waste, the population being killed and their houses destroyed, almost without exception. Large areas of Yorkshire were depopulated by massacre. This process, which became known as 'the harrying of the north', was effective in bringing that part of the country to heel. It demonstrated that no force in England could withstand the few thousand Norman knights at the King's disposal. The English risings also had the effect of hardening William's attitude towards the few Saxons remaining in authority. Thereafter Normans succeeded to practically every leading position in Church and State, including the appointment of the Norman Lanfranc to be Archbishop of Canterbury in 1070.

The final act of suppression came in 1071, when the King successfully besieged the Isle of Ely and put an end to the guerrilla warfare which had been carried on in East Anglia under the leadership of Hereward. The Norman Conquest, as a military operation, was complete. Thereafter William and his successors were to be more concerned with keeping their Norman barons in order than in suppressing Saxon risings. Indeed Saxons often came to be used to suppress rebellious Normans.

We can best round off the story of the Conquest with a brief description of the Norman feudal system as instituted by William in England.

There were many living in 1066 who could still remember the previous occasion when England had been under foreign rule. The twenty-six years of the three Danish Kings had seen an alien yoke applied in the mildest form, and no doubt many Englishmen believed, or at least hoped, that Norman rule would be similar. This, and the apparent invincibility of the Norman knights and their method of making war, was in large measure responsible for the wholesale submission of the English leaders of the south.

There is evidence that William's original intention was to exercise in England the comparatively moderate form of feudalism which had operated under the dukes of Normandy on the Continent, but on his return from Normandy in 1067 he seems to have changed his mind. There appear to have been two reasons for this. In the first place, as previously pointed out, the number of Saxon risings in the country—and in particular what he regarded as the treachery of earls Edwin and Morcar in the north—convinced him that a policy of appeasement was doomed to failure. Later the independent character, and discontent, shown by some of his own Norman followers decided him that a much firmer, and more centrally controlled, system of government was necessary than that in Normandy, if his own leading followers were to be kept in order.

The numerous local rebellions between 1067 and 1071 gave William the excuse for depriving English landlords of their estates and parcelling them out among his Norman followers. Eventually almost every shire was divided up among a total of some five thousand French-speaking knights,[1] who held their fees from French-speaking barons, or ecclesiastics, under the King.

The individual barons did not usually hold their land in one place: it was scattered about in various parts of the country. This clearly increased the King's authority, and enabled William to govern not solely through the barons, but partly through the sheriff of each shire. He also broke up the old earldoms—Wessex, Mercia and others—through which Saxon England had been governed.

In essence William governed through two separate channels—firstly, and indirectly, through his vassals, the feudal barons and prelates, and directly through the sheriffs—although the earldoms palatine of Chester and Shrewsbury and the county palatine of Durham were exceptions. The King also employed commissioners for special purposes, the most famous being those who carried out the Domesday survey. This system of rule did not meet with the approval of the Norman magnates, who had expected in England a form of feudal government similar to that in Normandy, and considered they had been deceived. This was the cause of the baronial rebellion of 1075, and many others in the history of the Norman kings.

The main feature of the feudal system was that it connected military service with the tenure of land, the core of Norman military power in England being the fortified castle and the mounted armoured knight.

Legally all land belonged to the King, who divided the country among his tenants-in-chief—the barons and leading Church dignitaries—who in return, and according

---

[1] The figure of five thousand, although only approximate, shows that the spoils of war were not confined to those knights who had fought at Hastings, as it is doubtful if as many as half that number survived the battle.

to the extent of their lands, had to provide so many fully equipped mounted knights for service in the field. These foreign rulers—scattered about an alien and potentially hostile country in comparatively small packets—naturally required protection in the form of secure bases. These were provided by the fortified castles which sprang up all over the country as the Conqueror's rule became effective.

The original castles, constructed soon after Hastings, were little more than wooden structures on some mound or hill, with a rough ditch or earthworks for their outer protection. Later these crude structures were greatly improved. The defended area might comprise some five to ten acres, the whole being surrounded by a moat with a high wall on the inner side. Inside this was another high wall, and inside that the 'keep', enclosed by the wall immediately surrounding the fortified stone castle. These edifices were built by forced English labour.

That, in the simplest terms, was the Norman castle— temporary in character and crude to start with, but later developing into well-built and extensive fortresses, some of which survive in a good state of preservation to this day. Used at first as protective bases by Normans against Saxons, they eventually became the strongholds of rival magnates, or fortresses to defy even the king, with English men-at-arms forming part of their garrisons. But that is another story: as Norman bases, for protection against a hostile population, and as headquarters for the first rough form of rule in the early days of the Conquest, they were impregnable against any forces which the English could muster.

Today the word 'feudal' is used to describe any system deemed out of date, barbarous or unjust. Yet—in those

days of poor communications, illiteracy and lack of homo-
geneity—feudalism was the most practical, indeed the only,
way of governing a country the size of England. It was open
to abuse and, like our own democratic system, was far from
perfect; but on the whole it served the country well and
was the first stage in our progress to become the leading
nation of the world by the nineteenth century. As G. M.
Trevelyan has put it: 'In this way the Dark Ages progressed
into the Middle Ages, and barbarism grew into civilization
—but decidedly not along the path of liberty and equality.'[1]

THE ULTIMATE INFLUENCE

The battle of Hastings has been likened to that at Waterloo
nearly 750 years later. The likeness is not, in my view, very
striking, but I agree that tactically there is some similarity.
Wellington fought the battle as Harold had hoped to do.
He allowed the French to batter themselves to pieces on the
British squares and then, judging the moment to a nicety,
by a wave of his hat, advanced his whole line to complete
the enemy's destruction. The difference was that *his* line
held against all the enemy's assaults and Harold's did not,
and Harold had no Blücher to attack the enemy in flank at
a critical stage of the battle.

In terms of tactics, therefore, there *is* some similarity if
one reverses the fortunes of the attackers and defenders; but
strategically, and in their long-term influence on affairs, the
two battles are poles apart. If Napoleon had won and
Wellington and Blücher had lost at Waterloo, it is tolerably
certain that twenty years later it would have made little
difference, and the world, as we know it today, would be

[1] *A Short History of England,* Introduction to Book Two.

much the same. Their defeat would have been a setback for the Allies and a short respite for Napoleon; but the former would have continued the fight and won in the end. Hastings, as we have seen, was a very different affair. With Harold's defeat there was nothing left to continue the struggle. The history of England was drastically changed and, in view of the leading role of England and the British Empire centuries later, its effect was clearly world wide.

In short, Waterloo was an incident of small ultimate importance: Hastings was a battle for a lasting kingdom with immense long-term consequences.

The remaining pages of this chapter are pure surmise. They are an attempt to indicate what might have happened if the fortunes of war had gone differently in 1066—if Harold could have arranged the battle more on the lines of Wellington in 1815. Although it is pure guesswork, it will be apparent that it contains some degree of probability and, as a mental exercise, is worth while if only to draw attention to the very great significance of the battle of Hastings— possibly one of the most important single day's work in recorded history.

In the eleventh century the twenty-one miles of the English Channel offered a much greater barrier than the far larger expanse of the North Sea, which separated England from Scandinavia. At this period the peoples of the main European land mass were not great sailors. Rival princes strove for power in innumerable petty wars; new dynasties were springing up, and a new form of warfare, based on feudalism and the mailed and mounted knight, was becoming fashionable. Under the influence of a re-invigorated and centralizing papacy, the Church was playing an increasingly important role in political affairs.

Continental Europe was absorbed with its own problems. In these conditions William's invasion of England was an affair in isolation, carried out only because of his special position—as rightful successor to the Confessor, as he undoubtedly believed he was—a belief itself fired by William's own quite outstanding personality. Had it ended in failure and disaster—and it was a fairly close-run thing— it seems unlikely that any further attempts at invasion from continental Europe would have been made, at least for a long time. On the other hand, the raids on the English coast, and settlement in the country, from Scandinavia, had been going on for centuries and might well have continued and indeed increased in scope.

If this is a correct picture of what might have been, it is not unreasonable to suppose that England would have remained a Nordic country, with a Nordic language and culture, remaining slightly aloof from the mainstream of European ideas and events, possibly with an increasingly Scandinavian orientation. Though feudalism of a sort might well have evolved eventually—and, indeed, showed signs of so doing before the Conquest—it is extremely unlikely that it would ever have been the efficient system so ruthlessly imposed by a victorious William on a conquered country, with a success and thoroughness which he and his prede-cessors and successors were quite unable to achieve in Normandy itself. The vigorous rule of the Norman and Plantagenet kings, the flood of ideas and techniques from the Continent, the eventual growth of the English language and character as we now know them—all these would never have occurred. In all probability England would have had the running sores of a hostile Wales and Scotland on her frontiers for much longer than was actually the case; and

Ireland might have remained the preserve of Celtic prince-
lings and Scandinavian pirates for centuries more. The Act
of Union of 1603 might never have taken place (or might
even, so to speak, have happened in reverse, with domination
of the south from the north), and there might never have
been a Great Britain or a United Kingdom.

Whatever its ultimate national benefits, 1066 was
undoubtedly an unprecedented disaster, so far as the ruling
caste of Anglo-Saxon England was concerned. What
remained of it after Hastings was rapidly deprived of its
land, position and opportunities. Only in the Church were
there still openings for non-Normans, and these were
limited in practice, for the Conqueror's centralizing policies
extended there too, and Normans and Norman protégés
were imported to fill the most important ecclesiastical
positions. Even the ordinary peasant suffered a loss of
status under Norman feudalism, and while hardship and
brutality had always been an accepted part of Anglo-Saxon
life, the Conqueror's rigid application of the Forest Laws
and his organized and far-reaching savagery when repress-
ing rebellion, be it large or small, undoubtedly intensified
the miseries of the ordinary people. For 150 years the native
population of England was very much a subject race. A
culture unique in Europe, and superior in artistry to that
of the Normans, withered overnight. A language of great
literary potential became regarded as fit only for serfs. The
Anglo-Saxon genius for compromise, the relatively easy
pace of Anglo-Saxon life, which had existed even amid the
harsh realities of eleventh-century living, the vision and
almost inconsequential whimsicality which had produced a
succession of remarkable missionaries, mystics and anony-
mous artists and craftsmen, were crushed under the weight

of Norman efficiency, organization and preference for the practical and the prosaic. Even the Norman saints have a common stamp of severity and even dullness beside their often riotously individualistic Anglo-Saxon counterparts!

Perhaps Normandy itself, too, was something of a loser at Hastings. William and his immediate descendants continued to regard it, and not England, as their true home— it is always something of a surprise to the modern Englishman to see William's tomb at Caen and not in Westminster Abbey, and the Bayeux Tapestry actually at Bayeux rather than in the British Museum! But their English preoccupations must have had a fundamentally adverse effect on their continental involvements. Who knows—had William been repulsed at Hastings, he or his successors might well have concentrated all future Norman energies on the French mainland, and France might have found her ultimate unity under a sovereign of the House of Normandy, not Capet. As it was, 1066 was Normandy's last great moment of international importance. After it, its most vigorous leaders were drawn away, either to England or to other spectacular but less enduring feats in Italy, the Aegean and Palestine, and Normandy fell into permanent political oblivion.

When the fusion of Anglo-Saxons and Normans in England eventually took place—and it was a process whose completion took several centuries—the result was a nation possessing certain distinctive features not found anywhere else in Europe. English institutions; the English system of government; the English language, product of the eventual blending of Anglo-Saxon and Norman-French; the English character, with its curious combination of Saxon vision and Saxon lethargy and Norman practicality and drive—all these must surely trace their own particular evolution from the change in direction so brusquely effected by the events of 14th October 1066.

The houses of Normandy, Blois and Anjou ruled England for more than four hundred years. During the whole of this period English interests were continuously directed towards Europe, and one of the main activities of Englishmen was to wage war on the continent of Europe in the interests of their sovereigns of continental extraction. These activities diminished with the accession in 1485 of the first of the Tudor monarchs, and thereafter the English gradually turned their eyes away from Europe and began to look farther afield. By this time, however, other countries—Spain and Portugal in particular—had begun to explore the oceans and colonize the New World. Columbus discovered Jamaica in 1492 and touched the mainland of America in 1498. The Cabots visited Newfoundland in 1497 and in the same year Vasco di Gama doubled the Cape of Good Hope. By 1519 Cortés had conquered Mexico. The exploration of the world beyond Europe, by Europeans, had begun, but England was to be a late starter. It was not until the loss of Calais in 1558 that the English finally turned away from continental Europe, and it was to be another twenty years before the great English sea-captains arose to challenge the continental adventurers. In 1576–8 Frobisher made three voyages to discover a north-west passage, in 1578–80 Drake sailed round the world, and in 1585–7 Davis made three voyages to Baffin Bay. The process of overseas settlement by Englishmen began in 1587 when Raleigh sent out 150 colonists to Virginia. In 1600 the East India Company was formed, and in 1614 the company's fleet defeated the Portuguese off the coast of India near Surat. In 1620 the Pilgrim Fathers landed in New England from the

Mayflower. During the next two hundred years England went on to found a civilization, but lose an empire, in North America, and to gain empires in India, Africa, Australia and New Zealand, culminating in the enjoyment, for a century, of the position of the most powerful nation in the world.

Some historians have suggested that the Norman Conquest, by producing a line of kings with dual nationality, directed English interests towards the continent of Europe to England's detriment as a sea-going nation. They maintain that the Nordic races were pre-eminently seafaring, and that without the Normans England would have been even earlier in the race for overseas discoveries and colonization. Others, opposed to these opinions, consider that without the energy, skill and organized government introduced by the Normans, England would have remained a fundamentally disunited country for generations, even centuries, to come (as was the case in Scandinavia), beset by wars between rival barons, with no policy or firm central government, and with neither capacity for, nor interest in, colonial expansion.

Both these lines of argument have their flaws. Had William failed in his invasion attempt it does not necessarily follow that England would have remained a Saxon-Danish country for ever, though this, I would suggest, is a fairly reasonable assumption. There might have been some later successful invasion from France, or even Spain, though, given the state of continental Europe as we know it at the time, it is hardly conceivable that this could have been attempted before the thirteenth century at the earliest. It is, however, interesting to consider that, had Harold won at Hastings, North America might today be populated by

H

62750

peoples of predominantly French or Spanish descent, and perhaps split up into numerous states, like South America. India might have fallen to France or Portugal; Australia and New Zealand might have been colonized from Holland or even from Japan.

Speculation of this kind has endless fascination, and offers limitless permutations. In conjunction with the concrete evidence already listed, however, it does serve to illustrate the historical importance of the battle which took place on Senlac Hill on 14th October 1066—a battle whose significance is difficult to appreciate from its short duration and from the comparatively small numbers involved. It was, indeed, an event which drastically altered the course of history.

William I of England, Duke of Normandy, is not usually included in the list of founders of the British Empire. Perhaps this is a mistake: maybe his name should be at the top of the roll.

APPENDICES

Chronology

IMPORTANT DATES AND TIMINGS
1042 to 1087

1042–66. EDWARD I, THE CONFESSOR

1042 With the death of Hardicanute, Edward, known as the Confessor, became King of England, thus restoring the old Saxon line after three Danish kings.

1044 Edward's Norman upbringing led to the appointment
to of Robert, Abbot of Jumièges, to be Bishop of London
1051 and Archbishop of Canterbury, and so began the gradual infiltration of Normans into the high offices of Church and State. Owing to this influence Earl Godwin and his family were exiled.

1051 William, Duke of Normandy, visited England as the
or guest of the Confessor, and later claimed that during
1052 this visit the King had named him as his successor.

1052 Godwin and his family returned to England, regained their influence with the King and caused a temporary decline in Norman influence.

1053 Godwin died and his son Harold, the future king, became Earl of Wessex.

1063 Harold distinguishes himself as leader in the war against the Welsh.

About Harold, on a visit to Duke William in Normandy,
1064   is made prisoner by Guy of Ponthieu, but later is
       hospitably treated by the Duke. He is introduced to
       the Norman form of warfare and persuaded to swear
       an oath acknowledging William as the Confessor's
       rightful heir to the English throne.

1066   Edward the Confessor died on 5th January, and the
       Witan nominated Harold, Earl of Wessex, to succeed
       him as King of England.

5th JANUARY TO 14th OCTOBER 1066. HAROLD II

1066   On hearing of Harold's succession William decided
       to fit out an expedition to enforce his claim to the
       English throne.

August to September: William's expedition (said to comprise
       696 ships) held up on the Normandy coast by
       supposed 'contrary winds'.

Early September: Owing to discontent among the shire levies,
       and shortage of provisions, Harold had to disband
       most of the force which had been watching the south
       coast in anticipation of the Norman invasion. About
       the same time the fleet also ran out of provisions and
       had to be sent round to London to revictual and refit.

Mid-September: Harald Hardrada, King of Norway, and
       Harold of England's brother, Tostig, land on the
       Yorkshire coast with a large army, with the intention
       of seizing the crown for Hardrada.

20th September: Earls Edwin and Morcar defeated by the
       Norwegian king at Fulford, near York.

25th September: Harold heavily defeats the Norwegians at Stamford Bridge, Harald Hardrada and Tostig being killed.

28th September: William lands unopposed at Pevensey with some 11,000 men and 3,600 horses. On completing disembarkation moves to Hastings, where he constructs a fortified camp, collects supplies and devastates the countryside.

1st October: Harold, on hearing news of William's landing, leaves York for London.

About 6th October: Harold arrives in London and begins collecting and organizing a force to meet William.

13th October: Harold begins assembling his army on Senlac Hill, seven miles from Hastings, and the site of the battle of Hastings.

14th October: THE BATTLE OF HASTINGS

Dawn. The Norman army begins to leave camp at Hastings.

About 9 a.m. Norman deployment, 700 to 1,000 yards from English position, begins.

About 9.30 a.m. Norman attack begins.

9.30 a.m.–4.30 p.m. The battle proceeds, with short pauses, the Normans attacking and the English defending stoutly. English gradually worn down; Harold, his two brothers and the majority of the English leaders killed.

By 5 p.m. English army in flight and William and his men left masters of the field.

14th OCTOBER 1066 TO 1087. WILLIAM I, THE
CONQUEROR

1066 William crowned in London on Christmas Day.
Many leading Saxons make their submission to the
new king.

1068 The subjugation of southern England completed.

1069 William conducts a campaign in northern England
against the rebellious earls Edwin and Morcar,
during which large areas of Yorkshire are devastated
and their inhabitants massacred—the process known
as 'the harrying of the north'.

1070 The Norman, Lanfranc, made Archbishop of
Canterbury.

1071 William defeats Hereward, the last Saxon to remain
in open rebellion, in East Anglia. This virtually
completed the Norman Conquest. Thereafter the
King had more opposition from the Norman barons
than from his new English subjects.

1075 William suppressed a rising by the Norman barons.

1086 The Domesday Survey made.

1087 Death of William the Conqueror.

Sources of Information

The sources of information about the battle of Hastings, and the years before and after, are meagre; but nevertheless better than in many episodes of similar antiquity. They fall into three categories:

a. *The Bayeux Tapestry*, the remarkable pictorial survey of the events leading up to the battle and the battle itself, designed and worked soon after the event and clearly inspired by someone with a good knowledge of the story. As far as the physical appearance of the three kings is concerned the Tapestry is supplemented by coins of the period.

b. *The Old Chroniclers*, none of whom were eye-witnesses, and several of whom wrote many years after the event.

c. *Comparatively Modern Writers*, who have reconstructed the battle from the Bayeux Tapestry, the works of the old chroniclers and their own views on the probable course of events.

Many of the old English battlefields—such as Shrewsbury (1403) and some of those of the Civil War—remain much the same as when the battles took place. This is not so with Hastings. The great forest, the Weald, immediately to the north of Senlac Hill, no longer exists in recognizable form, although I think the rough line of demarcation between forest and open down country is still just recognizable on some air photographs. The eastern part of the battlefield, that is, the left flank of the English line of battle, and the centre, are completely built up and covered by the town of Battle, the abbey, other fringe buildings and by the railway line and station. In viewing the site, therefore, a great deal of imagination is required to get a mind-picture of what it was like in 1066. We are, however, fortunate in having the high altar of the abbey, which indicates with precision the centre and approximate extent of the English position.

A study of a bibliography of Hastings appears at first sight to show that very few accounts—old or modern—were written by men with knowledge or experience of military affairs. I hardly think, however, that this is a valid comment in the case of the old chroniclers. In those times war played an important part in everyday life, and the priesthood, responsible for practically all the old accounts, were not the least militant members of the community.

In spite of the changed conditions a visit to the site is essential to a serious study of the battle of Hastings.

THE BAYEUX TAPESTRY AND COINS

The so-called 'Bayeux Tapestry' is not in fact a tapestry: it is a piece of embroidery—the design being worked on the material and not woven into it, as is the case with a true tapestry. Nevertheless, long usage has sanctioned the name 'Tapestry' and we will continue to use it here.

The origin of the Tapestry—as regards date and place of production, and those involved in its design—is a matter of dispute, but is no more controversial than many others of the period discussed in this book. We can at once discard the implications of the name 'The Tapestry of Queen Matilda'—suggesting that it was worked by the Conqueror's queen and her ladies. It is most unlikely that they would have had the technical skill for such work; but it is quite possible that the Queen took an interest in it during the course of production. In this way it may well have acquired her name, in the same way as in more recent times a building, public park, ship, etc., is sometimes associated with, and given the name of, some notable who was in fact only remotely connected with it.

In his book, *The Book of the Bayeux Tapestry*, Hilaire Belloc expresses the view that the Tapestry is a twelfth-century work. He has two main reasons for this belief:

(a) The Tapestry exactly fits the nave of Bayeux Cathedral. Although the exact date of the nave is not known, its near-Gothic architecture places it as having been constructed after the First Crusade, which took place in 1096–9.

(b) The crown worn by Edward the Confessor at the beginning of the Tapestry is marked with the fleur-de-lis, and this signifies the twelfth and not the eleventh century.

On this evidence Belloc considers that the Tapestry dates some fifty years after the battle, which means that its production was within the lifetime of some people who took part in the battle and within the lifetime of many who had talked with participants. These two arguments merit serious attention, but I do not find them conclusive. It is conceivable that it is coincidence that the Tapestry fits the nave, although I agree that the coincidence would be remarkable and is highly unlikely. It is possible that the nave was adapted to fit the Tapestry, or that the Tapestry was slightly altered to fit the nave. I am not convinced that the Confessor's crown is in fact marked with the fleur-de-lis, or that the fleur-de-lis, or something very similar, was not of the late eleventh century.

The more general view—including that of Sir Eric Maclagan and Sir Frank Stenton—is that the work was done within twenty years of the events it describes, and that the Tapestry was made in England to the order of Bishop Odo of Bayeux. The militant bishop had taken a prominent part in the battle, and may well have been proud of his achievements; for a period after Hastings he was responsible for the administration of Kent, and it was in Kent that certain church houses existed which it is thought possessed the technique to do the embroidery. The Tapestry has a very obvious Norman bias and is clearly designed to show William's undoubted right to the English crown, the highly competent manner in which the expedition was organized and the valour of the Normans in the battle, with the English putting up sufficient resistance to show that it was no 'walk-over' victory for the Duke's men. The fact that the Tapestry ends abruptly with the battle gives some credence to the view that it was designed soon after Hastings, as a later production would surely have included William's crowning and other follow-up incidents attributable to the battle. Finally, Odo would naturally wish to perpetuate the memory of this great event in his life in his own cathedral at Bayeux, and this may be why the Tapestry was made to fit the nave—or the nave the Tapestry.

There can be no certainty, but I find it highly credible

that the Bayeux Tapestry was the idea of Odo, was designed soon after the battle of Hastings and probably made in England. I am more doubtful about its date of production (as distinct from its design). It may not have been easy to find people with the necessary skill and it is not difficult to think of other causes of delay. In any case it was an immense task which would take years to complete. Although I believe it to have been designed within perhaps twenty years of the battle, I think it quite likely that the work was not completed until some fifty years after. During this time minor alterations could have been made which might account for the Tapestry so exactly fitting the nave and for the pattern of the Confessor's crown. If this is correct it brings much closer together the contentions of Hilaire Belloc and the other authorities I have mentioned.

Whatever its origins the Bayeux Tapestry remains unique. There is no other example of a detailed pictorial record, nearly contemporary, concerning an incident of great importance of that period.

The subsequent history of the Tapestry is obscure. It is mentioned in the inventory of Bayeux Cathedral in 1476, but apart from that was completely lost sight of until early in the eighteenth century, when it was rediscovered by two French archaeologists—M. Lancelot and Dom Bernard de Montfaucon. In 1767 an account of it was first published in English, with illustration, and thereafter historians began to interpret and make use of it. In 1803 Napoleon had it brought to Paris, but it was later returned to Bayeux. In 1913 the Tapestry was housed in the former residence of the Bishop of Bayeux. Soon after the outbreak of war in 1939 it was moved to Le Mans; but when in 1944 the Allies invaded France the Germans took it to Paris, and when

Paris was liberated it was found safely housed in the
Louvre. Later it was returned to Bayeux.

The first part of the Tapestry deals with Harold's depar-
ture for Normandy at the behest of the Confessor, his cross-
Channel voyage, arrest and imprisonment by Guy of Ponthieu
and his subsequent adventures with William in Normandy.
Much is made of Harold's oath acknowledging William as
the Confessor's heir; indeed the whole of this part of the
Tapestry is clearly designed to prove William's claim to the
English throne and show Harold as a perjurer and usurper.

The second part portrays William's preparations for the
invasion—following news that Harold had been crowned
King on the Confessor's death—the sailing of the expedition, its arrival at Pevensey and move to Hastings.

The third, and last, part deals with the battle itself, from
the time the Duke left Hastings until the disintegration of
the English army on Harold's death left the Normans
masters of the field.

It is interesting that no mention is made of Harold's
preoccupation at Stamford Bridge at the time of William's
landing. To have mentioned that would have detracted
from the Norman victory by exposing the disadvantage
under which the English king fought at Hastings.

Valuable as the Tapestry is, as an overall picture of
events from about 1064 to October 1066 and with its wealth
of detail, we must not overlook the fact that it has a Norman
bias and has certain inaccuracies—how many we do not
know with certainty. It is, for instance, noticeable that the
Normans and English are dressed alike, whereas obviously
they were not. The reason for this may be that the housecarls are mostly portrayed and their dress may not have
been so very different from the Norman knights'. They were

the household troops and the English Court had been under Norman influence for more than twenty years. Again it may be Norman bias that the ill-armed shire levies are not conspicuous in the Tapestry; to show them as the bulk of the English army would have given the impression of too easy a victory for the Duke.

It would be interesting to know something of the physical appearance of the three individuals chiefly concerned in this story—Edward, Harold and William. Most people who have studied the period have pictures in their minds—the Confessor a patriarchal figure, old beyond his years and with a flowing beard; Harold comes to mind as a typical Scandinavian, tall, blond, full of vitality; William we prefer to depict as powerfully built but not tall, swarthy and with a cruel and crafty look. It may well be that these descriptions are near the mark, but they are not easy to confirm. They lived before the days of the press photographer, or even the portrait painter; our only clues come from the Tapestry and from coins.

The National Portrait Gallery in London has on display silver pennies embossed with the heads of the three kings, and enlargements of these are shown on Plate 1. They are all attributed to Theodoric, who is believed to have been the royal goldsmith to all three kings. To what extent they are accurate we do not know, but it is reasonable to suppose that they are at least crude facial likenesses.

The producers of the Bayeux Tapestry seem to have made an effort to give a good full-face likeness of Edward, which resembles that on the coin enlargement on Plate 1. These, together with our knowledge of the Confessor's character and mode of life, are no doubt responsible for the popular conception of his appearance, which is very likely correct.

In the cases of Harold and William the Tapestry is less helpful, as there does not seem to have been any attempt at accuracy. As for Harold, the embossment on the coin does not show the buoyant, impulsive figure we imagine him to have been; but the shortness of his reign, and his active life during it, may not have given the opportunity for a good likeness. On the other hand, the side-face illustration of William *does* bear some resemblance to the popular conception.

We must leave it at that. We can have our ideas about the appearances of the three kings, which in the case of Edward is probably correct, but with the other two is little more than guessing.

THE BAYEUX TAPESTRY—BIBLIOGRAPHY AND NOTES

The Book of the Bayeux Tapestry, by Hilaire Belloc (1914).

An admirable book showing the whole Tapestry in colour, with explanatory notes and an Introduction by the author.

The Bayeux Tapestry, by Sir Eric Maclagan (various editions between 1943 and 1953).

The Bayeux Tapestry, by Eric Maclagan.

(King Penguin Book) with the entire Tapestry portrayed; some plates in colour. The book includes a valuable twenty-page Introduction.

The Bayeux Tapestry, a comprehensive Survey, edited by Sir Frank Stenton (1957).

This is a superb book, with 150 coloured and black-and-white illustrations. It includes chapters on the Tapestry by Sir Frank Stenton, Simone Bertrand, George Wingfield

Digby, Charles H. Gibbs-Smith, Sir James Mann, John L. Nevinson and Francis Wormald.

Note: There is a full-size reproduction of the Tapestry displayed at the Victoria and Albert Museum, London, and an excellent copy (embroidered in 1885–6) in the Reading Museum and Art Gallery.

THE OLD CHRONICLERS

Historians, journalists and others who take an interest in recording events know how difficult it is to discover the truth. With all our modern facilities for recording recent events, mistakes can and do occur, and they are not all due to carelessness or bias.

Imagine then the much greater difficulties of the chroniclers who wrote in the eleventh and twelfth centuries. Their numbers were strictly limited as, with a few exceptions, only the priesthood was literate and only a few priests had the ability, or were given the opportunity, to write history. When describing military operations they were very rarely eye-witnesses; they could hardly ever rely on written accounts as few of the participants were capable of writing a report. They had to rely on verbal accounts which were likely to be highly coloured, if not deliberately false. If they wished to interview some particular individual it might mean several days' journey by horse or on foot. The writer himself was almost certainly biased, if not from inclination then because some leading figure on one side or the other was his patron. Moreover, in matters of this kind it was the custom of the times to be swayed by the heart rather than the head. In their way they were romantics.

I

The historians of those days had a difficult task, and the wonder is that they wrote as well as they did. Nevertheless we must not deceive ourselves into believing that they were reliable chroniclers. They were not, even when they did their best, and too often they had ulterior motives for not doing their best. In the case of the battle of Hastings the difficulties were perhaps greater than in most. They had to write of an action which lasted but a few hours and in which the victors had every incentive to laud their achievement and the vanquished to keep quiet. Indeed the slaughter among the English leaders was so great that it must have been difficult to find a reliable eye-witness. As a result all the near-contemporary accounts were written by Normans.

The bibliographies and notes which follow are not a complete list, but include those old records which I think modern writers have found most useful.

THE OLD CHRONICLERS—BIBLIOGRAPHY AND NOTES

Gesta Guilielmi II Ducis Normannorum et Regis Anglorum I, by William of Poitiers (1071–6).

'The Acts of William Duke of Normandy and King of England.' The author was not present at Hastings, but was the Conqueror's chaplain, and consequently likely to have first-hand, although heavily biased, information. It seems quite probable that he had a hand in designing the Tapestry.

Gesta Normannorum Ducum, by William of Jumièges (1070).

'The Acts of the Norman Dukes.' The author was a Norman monk. His account is good background reading, but very little is said about the actual battle.

De Bello Hastingensis Carmen, attributed to Guy of Amiens.

'The Song about the Battle of Hastings.' The authorship is in some doubt and its date probably between 1076 and 1129.

Poem Descriptive of a Tapestry, by Abbot Baudri of Bourguil (1099–1102).

A poem addressed to Adela, the Conqueror's daughter. Based mostly on Poitiers's account.

Note. The above are contemporary, or near contemporary, works. Others of later date are as follows:

Chronicon Ex Chronicis, by Florence of Worcester (about 1118, or earlier).

'The Chronicle of Chronicles.' Florence of Worcester has a reputation for accuracy.

The Chronicles of Henry of Huntingdon (1139–1150).

The only non-Norman account by a medieval writer.

Roman de Rou, by Robert Wace (1160).

A chronical history of the dukes of Normandy in the form of a poem. At one time this work was regarded as a prime source of information, but in recent years it has been recognized for what it is—a highly coloured romance of very doubtful accuracy. It was written nearly a hundred years after Hastings.

Gesta Regum Anglorum, by William of Malmesbury.

'The Acts of the Kings of England.' Written about 1120.

MODERN WRITERS

Modern historians, that is those who have written within the past hundred years or so, have had to rely for their facts on the old chroniclers; but, as I have tried to make clear, there were many factors which make the old records unreliable—sometimes in good faith, sometimes with intent. In my opinion some modern historians have placed too much reliance on the old records, and assumed to be facts many incidents which are, in my view, clearly in doubt.

With a few notable exceptions—which will be apparent from the bibliography which follows—the modern writers have been scholars rather than men of military experience. Without in any way wishing to belittle the splendid books which many of them have written, I think that, generally, they are open to criticism on two counts. First, they have devoted too much importance to the tactical side of the battle—too much to the actual fighting—and not enough to the political and strategic moves which preceded it. This point is emphasized in Chapters III, IV and V.

Second, I think that lack of military knowledge has led some authors to accept as truth many incidents which I find unconvincing or at least 'not proven'. I cannot, for instance, accept as a fact William's delay of six weeks owing to 'contrary winds'; it may have been so but it is not a certainty. Nor can I accept without reservation the story of the 'feigned retreat' attributed to the Normans. There are many other cases where a trained military mind can change, or cast doubt upon, accepted stories connected with this battle.

It is noticeable that those writers with military experience are less dogmatic than those lacking it. They are more prone to indicate what is likely, and what would have been practicable and sensible militarily, whilst admitting that their conclusions may be wrong.

MODERN WRITERS—BIBLIOGRAPHY AND NOTES

The Norman Conquest, by Professor Freeman (1869).

It is very long and detailed and, although regarded as authoritative at the time, its treatment of the battle of Hastings is not now so highly considered.

Foundations of England, by Sir James Ramsey (1898).

Battles of English History, by H. B. George (1895).

Royal Engineers Journal, an article by General James in the, (January 1907).

This is an excellent account, which can be seen in most military libraries.

William the Conqueror, by Sir Frank Stenton (1908).

History of the Anglo-Saxons, by R. H. Hodgkins (1935).

Anglo-Saxon England, by Sir Frank Stenton (1945).

The Battlefields of England, by Lieutenant-Colonel Alfred H. Burne (1950).

This book contains an excellent chapter on Hastings. Lieutenant-Colonel Burne was notable for the accuracy of his facts, and for his reconstruction of old battles by a process which he called 'I.M.P.'—'Inherent Military Probability'.

The Field of Hastings, by Lieutenant-Colonel Charles H. Lemmon (1957).

An excellent little book with a very good map. The author lived practically on the battlefield for a number of years and made an exhaustive study of the subject.

The Golden Warrior, by Hope Muntz (1948).

The story of King Harold told as an historical novel. Although there is no pretence that the details are true, they are not improbable. The book gives an excellent reconstruction of the atmosphere and 'feel' of the times.

William the Conqueror, by David Douglas (1964).

A full, excellent and modern biography.

Hastings and the Battle Area in 1966

A BRIEF GUIDE FOR VISITORS

GENERAL

The area of country concerned with the battle of Hastings is situated in east Sussex, some ten miles from the Kent border. Hastings itself, and its adjoining twin town of St Leonards-on-Sea, is on the coast about sixty-three miles south of London. The two together have a population of about 67,000, which is considerably increased during the summer holiday season. Battle, where the fight took place, is about seven miles to the north-west, and has some 4,500 inhabitants. Pevensey and Bulverhythe, the strip of coast where the Conqueror landed, are respectively about ten and three miles west of Hastings.

The area is an attractive one, not only for those who like the sea, but also for those who prefer rural inland country. A week or two, or even a few days, can provide a good combination of holiday and a peep into history. The district has other interesting historical associations besides those connected with the Norman Conquest.

This appendix is intended as a guide for those who have in mind visiting this historic battle-ground. It contains mostly the mundane details of modern life, but I have included a few remarks of general historical interest and also indicated where more detailed information is obtainable.

The two focal areas are Hastings (including the road leading to Battle), and the town of Battle and its abbey.

HASTINGS

At the time of the Norman invasion Hastings was a considerable port for handling the trade between continental Europe and England. It had been a base for the fleet which earlier guarded the south coast against pirates and other marauders from overseas. By A.D. 928 it was included among the towns with its own mint. About 1050 it was classified as one of the five ports known as the Cinque Ports —the other four being Romney, Hythe, Dover and Sandwich. All, except Dover, have long ago lost their commercial interests, but are important holiday resorts.

Early in the 1590's plans were made, and implemented, for constructing a harbour; but the work was completely destroyed in 1597 when that part of the south coast was visited by a violent storm coinciding with an exceptionally high tide.

In 1940 small boats from Hastings assisted in the evacuation of troops from Dunkirk, and later, in common with other towns and ports on that part of the coast, prepared for the German invasion—which did not materialize.

Most of the people who visit Hastings during the summer months are tourists; only a small proportion make the trip to Battle, or take an interest in the historic event which took place there nine hundred years ago. Yet one feels that a more inquisitive rising generation will have a greater interest in history and that more visitors will spend at least a part of their time looking round the battlefield and other places of historical importance. It is largely for such people that this section of the book has been written.

The visitor to Hastings travelling by rail from London has the choice of four stations—Charing Cross, Cannon Street, London Bridge and Victoria—the journey averaging slightly less than two hours. Trains run approximately once an hour, both ways, from about 7 a.m. to 10 p.m.

There is also a good coach service from London (Victoria Coach Station). Coaches leave at frequent intervals throughout the summer months, with a reduced service at other times of the year. The journey takes about $3\frac{1}{4}$ hours.

From Hastings there are local bus and coach services to most places of interest in the district.

The journey from London by private car takes about $2\frac{1}{2}$ to 3 hours; but may take longer at morning and evening 'rush hour' periods when there is traffic congestion in and out of London, and sometimes at places *en route* during the summer and at week-ends. No roads of any consequence were constructed in England between the time the Romans left and the Norman invasion, and most of those in existence were badly neglected. It is difficult to say how near the modern motorist from London travels to the route taken by Harold's men when marching to the battle. It is, however, tolerably certain that the present road between Hastings and Battle is approximately the same as the route used by William during his advance on the morning of 14th October 1066.

The Hastings Public Museum and Art Gallery in Johns' Place has an excellent model of the battle, and other relics of Saxon and early Norman times.

Information about other places of interest in and around
Hastings is obtainable from the Information Bureau at the
Town Centre, near the Memorial.

There are a number of hotels in and near the town
offering accommodation to suit most tastes and pockets.

BATTLE

For those who wish to see the battlefield of Hastings—
whether as casual sightseers or as serious students of
military history—the town of Battle, with its abbey, is the
focal point.

As explained earlier, the site of the battle is known
precisely, but due to modern buildings (noticeably the
town of Battle, the abbey and the railway), the planting of
trees and agricultural activities, it presents an entirely
different appearance from the battlefield of 1066. This
applies particularly to the left flank and centre of the
English position, which are entirely built over.

It is now impossible to view the whole battlefield from
any one point. In his excellent little book, *The Field of
Hastings*, Lieutenant-Colonel C. H. Lemmon gives seven
points which together give a view of the entire battlefield,
including the rear of the English position. They are all on
land open to the public. These points are all shown by
figures in a circle: thus, ②, on Map IV, for the benefit
of the serious student. But for the average viewer of the
battlefield I think the following three will suffice, and are
the most important.

a. *The west end of the Lower Terrace in the abbey grounds*
   (marked ⑤ on Map IV).

   From this viewpoint can be seen most of the western

flank of the battlefield, the right of the English position, and the ground over which the Bretons made their advance, and hasty retreat, in the early stage of the battle.

b. *At the south end of the road bridge over the railway, a track leading north-east to St Mary's Farm* (marked ① on Map IV).

From here can be seen part of the Caldbec Hill, including the Windmill, parts of the left of the English positions and parts of what was probably the Norman line of deployment. This viewpoint has become somewhat restricted owing to recent (1965) building.

c. *The southern outskirts of Battle, a few yards along Powdermill Lane* (marked ② on Map IV).

From this stand can be seen parts of the centre of the English position, and what is probably the line of deployment of the Norman centre—the division under the Duke and composed almost exclusively of Normans.

A careful survey from these three positions will give a good general idea of the battlefield. The visitor who can spare the time should also go to the spot on Telham Hill marked W.R. on Maps III and IV, which I think is probably the place from which Duke William made his reconnaissance and got his first view of the English army. On a clear day a good view is obtainable of the right and centre of Harold's position, and it gives a sense of satisfaction, and to most people a thrill, to stand on this historic spot.

Battle Abbey is open to the public and a guide takes visitors round. There are also a number of other interesting places in and around Battle.

Hotel accommodation is available in and near the town.

The journey from London by rail takes about $1\frac{1}{2}$ hours from Charing Cross, Waterloo or Cannon Street. Trains leave hourly, both ways, between about 7 a.m. and 11 p.m.

Coaches between London and Hastings stop at Battle, the journey from London taking about $2\frac{3}{4}$ hours.

LITERATURE

Apart from the historical works mentioned in Appendix B, the following literature is obtainable from the Hastings Information Bureau, or at Battle Abbey and elsewhere locally.

Outline of Hastings History, by J. Manwaring Baines (Curator of Hastings Museum).

Hastings Castle, by W. H. Dyer.

1066 and All This, by Peter Button.

Directory of Information (published periodically by the County Borough of Hastings).

Map of Hastings and St Leonards.

Battle Abbey, Sussex: an illustrated Historical Sketch, by Sir Harold Brakspear.

St Mary the Virgin's Church, Battle, a short history published under the authority of the dean and churchwardens.

Note. Some of the above are available free. A small charge is made for others.

INDEX

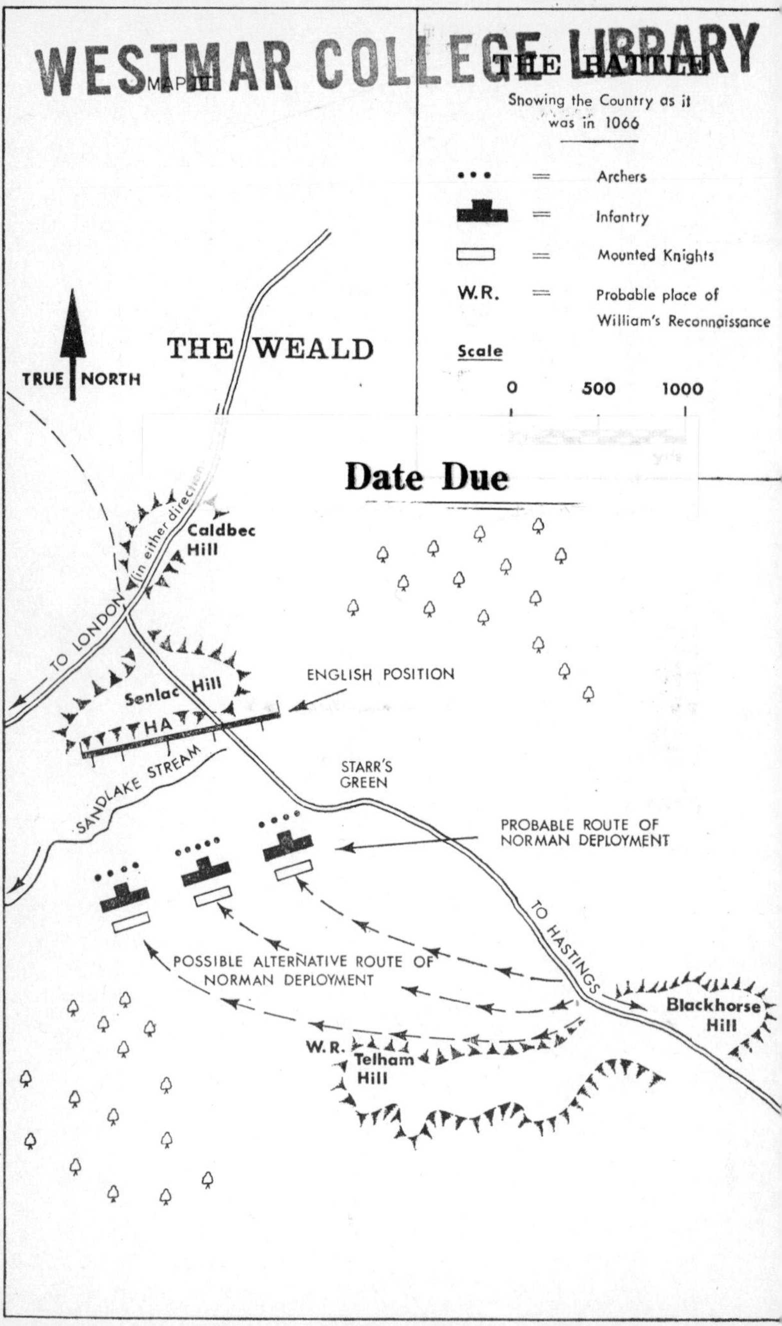
MAP II
THE BATTLE
Showing the Country as it was in 1066
• • • = Archers
= Infantry
= Mounted Knights
W.R. = Probable place of William's Reconnaissance
Scale
0
500
1000
THE WEALD
TRUE NORTH
TO LONDON
(in either direction)
Caldbec Hill
Senlac Hill
HA
ENGLISH POSITION
SANDLAKE STREAM
STARR'S GREEN
PROBABLE ROUTE OF NORMAN DEPLOYMENT
TO HASTINGS
POSSIBLE ALTERNATIVE ROUTE OF NORMAN DEPLOYMENT
Blackhorse Hill
W.R.
Telham Hill